TRIO
LISTENING
AND SPEAKING 2

The Intersection of
Vocabulary, Listening, & Speaking

Laurie Blass

OXFORD
UNIVERSITY PRESS

OXFORD
UNIVERSITY PRESS

198 Madison Avenue
New York, NY 10016 USA

Great Clarendon Street, Oxford, OX2 6DP, United Kingdom

Oxford University Press is a department of the University of Oxford.
It furthers the University's objective of excellence in research, scholarship,
and education by publishing worldwide. Oxford is a registered trade
mark of Oxford University Press in the UK and in certain other countries

© Oxford University Press 2017

The moral rights of the author have been asserted

First published in 2017

2021 2020 2019 2018 2017

10 9 8 7 6 5 4 3 2 1

ISBN: 978 0 19 420307 4 STUDENT BOOK 2 WITH ONLINE PRACTICE PACK
ISBN: 978 0 19 420304 3 STUDENT BOOK 2 AS PACK COMPONENT
ISBN: 978 0 19 420322 7 ONLINE PRACTICE WEBSITE

Printed in China

This book is printed on paper from certified and well-managed sources

ACKNOWLEDGEMENTS

Cover Design: Yin Ling Wong

Illustrations by: Ben Hasler, p.26, 44, 58, 84, 129; Joe Taylor, p.34, 53, 67, 72, 123.

The author and publishers are grateful to those who have given permission to reproduce the following: http://articles.latimes.com/2014/jan/02/autos/la-fi-hy-autos-ihs-autonomous-cars-study-20140102

The publishers would like to thank the following for their kind permission to reproduce photographs: p.1 oneinchpunch/Shutterstock, Keith Morris/age fotostock/Superstock, Cultura Limited/Superstock; p.3 Rob Lewine/Getty Images, The Chosunilbo JNS/Multi-Bits via Getty Images, Hero Images/Getty Images, Shutterstock/Santiago Cornejo, Shutterstock/Jochen Schoenfeld, Olga Langerova/Shutterstock, ARENA Creative/Shutterstock, Monkey Business Images/Shutterstock; p.6 Shotshop GmbH/Alamy Stock Photo, Peter ten Broecke/Getty Images, skynesher/Getty Images, StockLite/Shutterstock, Olga Danylenko/Shutterstock, Christian Bertrand/Shutterstock, Perart/Shutterstock, Anatoliy Cherkas/Shutterstock; p.19 Aflo Co. Ltd./Alamy Stock Photo, Radu Bercan/Shutterstock.com, Photographee.eu/Shutterstock; p.20 Hero Images Inc./Alamy Stock Photo, michaeljung/iStock/Getty Images Plus, kali9/Getty Images, Odua Images/Shutterstock, Vinne/Shutterstock, Photographee.eu/Shutterstock, Phovoir/Shutterstock, Cultura Limited/Superstock; p.22 lovleah/Getty images, Caiaimage/Robert Daly/Getty Images, Richard Smith/Masterfile, Andrey_Popov/Shutterstock, Photographee.eu/Shutterstock, Blend Images/Superstock, Blend Images/Superstock, Michael DeYoung/Alaska Stock - Design Pics/Superstock; p. 31 Hero Images/Getty Images; p.32 Tomas Abad/Alamy Stock Photo, Caryn Becker/Alamy Stock Photo, MoiseevVladislav/Getty Images, Glowimages/Masterfile, Radu Bercan/Shutterstock.com, zoff/Shutterstock, Andrey_Popov/Shutterstock, Image Source/Superstock; p.43 Hero Images/Getty Images; p.46 Aflo Co. Ltd./Alamy Stock Photo, REUTERS/Alamy Stock Photo, ESB Professional/Shutterstock, Anna Hoychuk/Shutterstock.com, Andrei Kholmov/Shutterstock.com, Sorbis/Shutterstock.com, Boiarkina Marina/Shutterstock, Blend Images/Superstock; p.50 Chris Willson/Alamy Stock Photo, AFP/AFP/Getty Images, Andreas Rentz/Getty Images, Hero Images/Getty Images; p.57 Lev Dolgachov/Alamy Stock Photo, Thomas Barwick/Getty Images, Aurora Photos/Masterfile; p. 60 Lev Dolgachov/Alamy Stock Photo, JulNichols/Getty Images, Nick Onken/Masterfile, Garsya/Shutterstock, Dmitry Molchanov/Shutterstock, Andrey_Popov/Shutterstock; p.69 Hero Images/Getty Images; p.70 Image Source/Getty Images, Ariel Skelley/Getty Images, VINCENZO PINTO/AFP/Getty Images, Thomas Barwick/Getty Images; p.81 Hero Images/Getty Images; p. 82 Peter Titmuss/Alamy Stock Photo, William Bunce/Alamy Stock Photo, Aurora Photos/Masterfile, R. Tyler Gross/Aurora Open/Superstock; p.9 Hero Images/Getty Images; p.95 Manfred Gottschalk/Alamy Stock Photo; Aflo Relax/Masterfile; Yoko Aziz/age fotostock/Superstock; p.96 Sri Maiava Rusden/Getty Images, Elena Elisseeva/Shutterstock, Blue Jean Images/Superstock, agf photo/Superstock; p.98 Charles Bowman/Axiom Photographic/AGE Fotostock, robertharding/Alamy Stock Photo, Craig Lovell/Getty Images, robertharding/Masterfile, Gerard Lacz Images / Superstock, Aflo Relax/Masterfile, Benny Marty/Shutterstock.com, Olga Danylenko/Shutterstock; p.107 Hero Images/Getty Images; p.108 Didier ZYLBERYNG/Alamy Stock Photo, Manfred Gottschalk/Alamy Stock Photo, Shutterstock/r.nagy, Shutterstock/Viacheslav Lopatin, Shutterstock/Jason Patrick Ross, orlandin/Shutterstock, age fotostock/Superstock, DeAgostini/Superstock; p. 110 keith morris/Alamy Stock Photo, Adrian Sherratt/Alamy Stock Photo, Danita Delimont/Alamy Stock Photo, David McNew/Getty Images, Shutterstock/FloridaStock, Shutterstock/dibrova; p.113 Shutterstock/aphotostory, Waj/Shutterstock, Anton_Ivanov/Shutterstock; p. 119 Hero Images/Getty Images; p.120 Aurora Photos/Alamy Stock Photo, keith morris/Alamy Stock Photo, Jeff Rotman/Getty Images, PhotoVic/Getty Images, Paul Nicklen/National Geographic/Getty Images, goodluz/Shutterstock, Yoko Aziz/age fotostock/Superstock, imageBROKER/Superstock; p.122 Dave Stamboulis/AGE Fotostock, dbimages/Alamy Stock Photo, Hector Chapman/Alamy Stock Photo, Dreamframer/Getty Images, Witold Skrypczak/Getty Images, LeoPatrizi/Getty Images; p.131 Hero Images/Getty Images.

REVIEWERS

We would like to acknowledge the following individuals for their input during the development of the series:

Aubrey Adrianson
Ferris State University
U.S.A.

Sedat Akayoğlu
Middle East Technical University
Turkey

Mahmoud Al-Salah
University of Dammam
Saudi Arabia

Lisa Alton
University of Alberta
Canada

Robert J. Ashcroft
Tokai University
Japan

Ibrahim Atay
Izzet Baysal University
Turkey

Türkan Aydin
Çanakkale Onsekiz Mart University
Turkey

Pelin Tekinalp Cakmak
Marmara University, School of Foreign Languages
Turkey

Raul Cantu
Austin Community College
United States

Karen E. Caldwell
Higher Colleges of Technology, Women's College, U.A.E.

Danielle Chircop
Kaplan International English
U.S.A.

Jennifer Chung
Gwangju ECC
South Korea

Elaine Cockerham
Higher College of Technology
Oman

Abdullah Coskun
Abant Izzet Baysal University
Turkey

Stephanie da Costa Mello
Glendale Community College
U.S.A.

Travis Cote
Tamagawa University
Japan

Linda Crocker
University of Kentucky
U.S.A.

Ian Daniels
Smart ELT
Japan

Adem Onur Fedai
Fatih University Preparatory School
Turkey

Gail Fernandez
Bergen Community College
U.S.A.

Theresa Garcia de Quevedo
Geos Boston English Language School
U.S.A.

Greg Holloway
Kyushu Institute of Technology
Japan

Elizabeth Houtrow
Soongsil University
South Korea

Shu-Chen Huang
National Chengchi University
Taipei City

Patricia Ishill
Union County College
U.S.A.

Ji Hoon Kim
Independence English Institute
South Korea

Masakazu Kimura
Katoh Gakuen Gyoshu High School/Nihon University
Japan

Georgios-Vlasios Kormpas
Al Yamamah University/SILC
Saudi Arabia

Ece Selva Küçükoğlu
METU School of Foreign Languages
Turkey

Ji-seon Lee
Jeong English Campus
South Korea

Sang-lee Lee
Kangleong Community Language Center
South Korea

Zee Eun Lim
Reader's Mate
South Korea

James MacDonald
Aspire Language Academy
Kaohsiung City

Margaret Martin
Xavier University
U.S.A.

Murray McMahon
University of Alberta
Canada

Chaker Ali Mhamdi
Al Buraimi University College
Oman

Elizabeth R. Neblett
Union County College
U.S.A.

Eileen O'Brien
Khalifa University of Science, Technology and Research
U.A.E.

Fernanda Ortiz
Center for English as a Second Language at University of Arizona
U.S.A.

Ebru Osborne
Yildiz Technical University
Turkey

Joshua Pangborn
Kaplan International
U.S.A.

John Peloghitis
Tokai University
Japan

Erkan Kadir Şimşek
Akdeniz University Manavgat Vocational College
Turkey

Veronica Struck
Sussex County Community College
U.S.A.

Clair Taylor
Gifu Shotoku Gakuen University
Japan

Melody Traylor
Higher Colleges of Technology
U.A.E.

Whitney Tullos
Intrax
U.S.A.

Sabiha Tunc
Baskent University English Language Department
Turkey

John Vogels
Dubai Men's College
U.A.E.

Pingtang Yen
Eden Institute
Taichung City

Author Acknowledgments

Many thanks to Alice Savage and Colin Ward, the originators of this series, for their inspiration and creativity. I am also very grateful to Sandra Frith, Eliza Jensen, Karin Kipp, and the Oxford University Press editorial and design staff for all their hard work on this project.

—L.B.

CONTENTS

UNIT 2 Health and Wellness *(continued)*

CHAPTER	▲ VOCABULARY	▲▲ LISTENING	▲▲▲ SPEAKING
6 **What Was It Like?** page 82	Oxford 2000 🗝 words to talk about healthy environments	Listening for ways speakers show interest and understanding Listening for problems and solutions	Link *was/wasn't/were/weren't* with vowels Describing how a change made life better, safer, or healthier

UNIT WRAP UP **Extend Your Skills** page 94

UNIT 3 Travel and Tourism pages 95–132

CHAPTER	▲ VOCABULARY	▲▲ LISTENING	▲▲▲ SPEAKING
7 **Where Were You Going?** page 96	Oxford 2000 🗝 words to talk about travel	Listening for tone and attitude Listening to take notes with a mind map	Linking *wh-* questions words with *was/were* Describing an unusual or surprising travel experience
8 **Why Should You Go There?** page 108	Oxford 2000 🗝 words to talk about important places	Listening for specific details Listening for causes and effects	Reducing *have to* and *has to* Describing an important place and explaining why we should protect it
9 **Who Gave It to You?** page 120	Oxford 2000 🗝 words to talk about adventure	Recognizing promotional language Listening to take notes with a T-chart	Practicing sentence stress Presenting a position in a debate

UNIT WRAP UP **Extend Your Skills** page 132

The Oxford 2000 🗝
List of Keywords

Welcome to Trio Listening and Speaking

Building Better Communicators . . . From the Beginning

Trio Listening and Speaking includes three levels of Student Books, Online Practice, and Teacher Support.

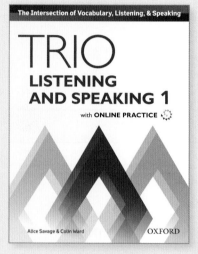

Level 1/CEFR A1

Level 2/CEFR A2

Level 3/CEFR B1

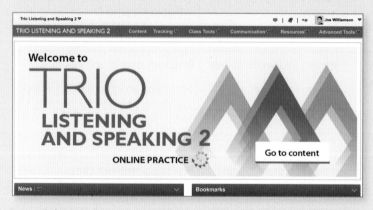

Essential Digital Content with Classroom Resources for Teachers

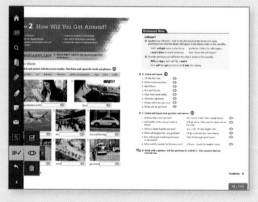

Classroom Presentation Tool

Trio Listening and Speaking's contextualized vocabulary instruction, academic listening strategies, and focus on pronunciation provide students with the tools they need for successful academic listening and speaking at the earliest stages of language acquisition.

Vocabulary Based On the Oxford 2000 🔑 Keywords

Trio Listening and Speaking's vocabulary is based on the 2,000 most important and useful words to learn at the early stages of language learning, making content approachable for low-level learners.

Practical Listening and Speaking Instruction

Conversation and academic listening sections prepare learners for real situations, while a focus on pronunciation helps students communicate successfully.

Readiness Unit

For added flexibility, each level of *Trio Listening and Speaking* begins with an optional Readiness Unit to provide fundamental English tools for beginning students.

INSIDE EACH CHAPTER

▲ VOCABULARY

Theme-based chapters set a context for learning.

Essential, explicit skills help beginning learners to gain confidence with listening and speaking.

The Grammar Note is matched closely to the listening and speaking tasks for supportive grammar instruction.

Vocabulary is introduced in context and is built from the Oxford 2000 list of keywords.

Trio Listening and Speaking Online Practice extends learning beyond the classroom, providing students with additional practice and support for each chapter's vocabulary, grammar, and skills instruction.

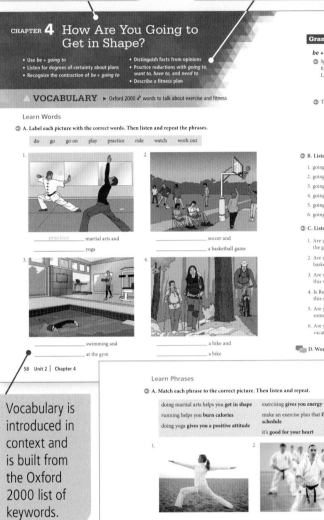

▲▲ LISTENING

Sounds of English boxes provide sound-symbol decoding practice, and link fluency with listening and speaking skills to improve students' understanding of how English is really spoken.

Vocabulary and Grammar Chants found online help students internalize the target grammar structure and vocabulary for greater fluency when listening and speaking.

Conversation activities help students practice words, phrases, and grammar used in everyday situations.

Academic Listening prepares students for academic life.

Listening Strategies give students the techniques they need to listen effectively.

▲▲ LISTENING

CONVERSATION

A. Listen to the conversation. Who is going to be more active this weekend? Circle the correct name.

Mariko   Andy

B. Listen to the conversation again. What activities are Mariko and Andy going to do this weekend? Check (✓) the correct answers.

☐ watch TV   ☐ get some sleep

☐ go swimming   ☐ take a martial arts class

☐ take an exam   ☐ go on a bike ride

☐ study for an exam   ☐ go on a hike

Listening Strategy

Listening for degrees of certainty about plans

Speakers use words to show how certain they are about plans. Listen to the examples.

More certain ⟶ Less certain

absolutely definitely probably maybe

You're **absolutely** going to love this new phone! It has some great apps.

Luis is **definitely** going to apply for that job. He really wants to work with kids.

She's **probably** going to work this summer. She doesn't want to go to school.

Maybe I'll take Spanish next year. Or **maybe** I'll take Italian.

GO ONLINE for more practice

C. Listen to parts of the conversation again. Complete the sentences with the words in the box. Responses may be used more than once.

| absolutely | definitely | maybe | probably |

1. Andy: I'm _____probably_____ going to hang around my apartment.

2. Andy: What about you? Are you going to relax?

   Mariko: _____ not! I'm going to get some fresh air and exercise.

3. Mariko: Yep. I'm _____ going to take a martial arts class on Saturday, then I'm going to go on a long bike ride.

4. Mariko: And _____ I'll go swimming on Sunday.

5. Andy: Well, I don't know about you, but I'm _____ going to feel better by Monday morning. I'm staying right here on the couch.

Sounds of English

Contraction of be + going to

Speakers usually use contractions with be + going to. They contract the subject and be in the affirmative. They contract be with not in the negative. Listen to the examples.

I am going to ride my bike. → **I'm** going to ride my bike.

She is going to graduate next year. → **She's** going to graduate next year.

We are going to take the subway. → **We're** going to take the subway.

D. Listen and check (✓) the phrase you hear.

1. ☑ they are going to go   ☐ they're going to go

2. ☐ he is going to come   ☐ he's going to come

3. ☐ she is going to get   ☐ she's going to get

4. ☐ I am going to see   ☐ I'm going to see

5. ☐ he is going to take   ☐ he's going to take

6. ☐ we are going to play   ☐ we're going to play

E. Work with a partner. Partner A asks about next summer. Partner B answers. Focus on pronouncing contracted forms of be + going to. Then partners switch roles.

Partner A		Partner B	
What are you	going to get?	I'm	going to...
What is your family	going to do?	They're	
What is your sister	going to see?	He's	
What is your brother		She's	

Chant

GO ONLINE for the Chapter 4 Vocabulary and Grammar Chant

ACADEMIC LISTENING

A. Check (✓) the reasons people exercise. Add your own ideas. Share your ideas with a partner.

☐ for fun

☐ to lose weight

☐ to get strong

☐ to relax

☐ _____

☐ _____

B. Listen to the first section of the show. Circle the topic of the show.

the benefits of exercise   different types of exercise   exercise mistakes

C. Listen to the first and second sections of the show. Circle the correct answer to each question.

1. Does exercise help you lose weight?   It helps you a little bit.   It doesn't help you at all.

2. What happens when people exercise? They burn calories at   the end of   the beginning of an exercise program.

3. How do we know this?   Researchers   Lucia Suarez   did a study at City University of New York.

4. The research shows that you might lose weight when you   start   stop an exercise program.

Listening Strategy

Distinguishing facts from opinions

A fact is something that a person can prove, for example, with an experiment. An opinion is an idea. No one proved it, but someone might prove it in the future. Speakers use prove, show, and find to introduce a fact. They use think and believe to introduce an opinion. Listen to the examples.

Some people **think** exercise helps you lose weight.   This is just an idea.

However, a study **showed** that exercise does not always burn calories.   A study proved this.

GO ONLINE for more practice

D. Listen to the third section of the show. Complete each sentence with the word you hear.

| believe | show | showed | think |

1. Most experts _____ that exercise has a lot of emotional benefits.

    F   O

2. Some studies _____ that people felt happier and more relaxed when they exercised regularly.

    F   O

3. Many studies _____ that exercise is good for your heart.

    F   O

4. Some experts also _____ that people who exercise don't get sick as often as people who don't exercise.

    F   O

E. Work with a partner. Are the underlined ideas in Activity D facts or opinions? Circle F for fact or O for opinion.

F. Listen to the show again. Ask and answer the questions with a partner.

Partner A	Partner B
1. Does exercising always help you lose weight?	2. Who did a study about exercising and weight loss?
3. When does exercising help you lose weight?	4. What is the best way to make an exercise plan?
5. What is one benefit of exercising?	6. What is another benefit of exercising?

Discuss the Ideas

G. What are some reasons people don't exercise? Check (✓) the problems and add your own idea.

☐ They don't have time.   ☐ It hurts.

☐ It costs too much money.   ☐ It's boring.

☐ It doesn't help them lose weight.   ☐ _____

H. Work with a partner. Think of solutions for the problems in Activity G.

SPEAKING

> The Pronunciation Skill helps students to speak clearly and intelligibly.

SPEAKING

Speaking Task Describing a fitness plan

Step 1 PREPARE

Pronunciation Skill

Reduction of going to, want to, have to, and need to

Speakers often combine and shorten verb phrases with *to* such as *going to*, *want to*, *have to*, and *need to*. Listen to the examples.

I'm **going to** leave soon.	→	I'm **gonna** leave soon.
Do you **want to** go with us?	→	Do you **wanna** go with us?
I **have to** see this.	→	I **hafta** see this.
What do you **need to** do?	→	What do you **needta** do?

GO ONLINE for more practice

A. Listen and check (✓) the sentence you hear.

1. [✓] We're going to get some sleep.   [ ] We're gonna get some sleep.
2. [ ] I have to get some fresh air.   [ ] I hafta get some fresh air.
3. [ ] When do you want to go swimming?   [ ] When do you wanna go swimming?
4. [ ] They want to lose some weight.   [ ] They wanna lose some weight.
5. [ ] He's going to fall asleep on the couch.   [ ] He's gonna fall asleep on the couch.
6. [ ] Do you need to buy a new car?   [ ] Do you needta buy a new car?

B. Listen and repeat the questions and answers.

1. What are you going to do this weekend?   I'm going to work out at the gym.
2. When do you want to take a vacation?   We want to take a vacation next spring.
3. Where do you want to go?   We want to go to San Diego.
4. What do you have to do this evening?   I have to do chores around the house.
5. Where do you have to go tomorrow?   I have to go downtown.
6. What do you need to do before an exam?   I need to read the textbook.

C. Work with a partner. Partner A asks a question from Activity B. Partner B gives the answer. Then partners switch roles.

D. Listen. Complete the conversation with the phrases you hear. Responses may be used more than once.

going to	have to	need to	want to

A: So, Miles, what are you _____ going to _____ do this summer?
B: I'm _____ get a job.
A: A job?
B: Yeah, I _____ make some money so I can buy a new car.
A: So, what kind of job do you _____ get?
B: I _____ find a job that pays well.
A: That makes sense.
B: And we worked out all year at the gym, so I _____ keep fit, too.
A: Good idea. So, what kind of job do you think you'll find?
B: My uncle owns a gym. I'm _____ ask him for job.
A: Fantastic! So you can work out and make money at the same time.
B: That's the idea. So, what about you? What are you _____ do this summer?
A: Same here. I _____ keep fit, too, so I'm _____ get a job at the pool.
B: Sounds like we'll both be in good shape next fall.

GO ONLINE to practice the conversation

E. Work with a partner. Practice the conversation in Activity D.

> Carefully staged speaking tasks build student confidence.

66 Unit 2 | Chapter 4   Speaking 67

Step 2 SPEAK

A. Some people want to get in shape outside of a gym. What are some interesting ways to do this? Write your ideas in the first column in the chart.

Ways to keep fit	Who will this work for?	Benefits (Why will this work?)

B. Who will your fitness ideas work for? Think about different groups of people such as students, workers, parents, and so on. Write your ideas in the middle column in the chart in Activity A.

C. Work with a partner. Think about three benefits for each way to get in shape in the chart in Activity A. Add your ideas to the third column.

> Speaking Skills boxes provide explanations of expressions frequently used in spoken English to improve students' natural-sounding speech.

Word Partners

be fit
get fit
keep fit
look fit
stay fit

GO ONLINE to practice word partners

Speaking Skill

Describing benefits

When speakers describe a plan, they explain how the plan will benefit people. They show the good things about the plan. Speakers use examples and reasons to explain benefits. Listen to the examples.

Our fitness plan has many benefits. For example, *it will work for busy people* because *it only takes 15 minutes a day. It's also inexpensive* because *people don't need any special equipment with our plan*.

D. Work with a partner. Use the chart in Activity A and the examples in the Speaking Skill box. Partner A asks about the benefits of the ways to keep fit. Partner B describes one benefit. Then partners switch roles.

Partner A	Partner B
How will...benefit students? workers? parents?	It will benefit...because...

Speaking Task

Describing a fitness plan

1. Look at your notes in Step 2. Choose one way to keep fit. Explain how it will work and who it's for. Make a list of benefits. Organize your ideas in the chart.

My fitness plan	Who is this for?	Benefits

2. Close your book. Work in a group. Describe your plan to your group. Ask your group members questions about their plans.

Step 3 REPORT

A. Write sentences about your group members' plans. Then discuss what plan will work the best and why.

Name	Plan description	Benefits

B. Work with a new partner. Describe the plan you want to try. Why do you want to try it?

Step 4 REFLECT

Checklist

Check (✓) the things you learned in Chapter 4.
○ I learned language to describe a fitness plan.
○ I understood a conversation about exercise plans.
○ I described a fitness plan for a particular group of people.

Discussion Question

What are some other ways to stay healthy, especially for students?

> Students discuss a question in small groups to develop critical thinking skills.

68 Unit 2 | Chapter 4   Speaking 69

ix

Trio Listening and Speaking Online Practice: Essential Digital Content

Trio Listening and Speaking Online Practice provides multiple opportunities for skills practice and acquisition—beyond the classroom and beyond the page.

Each unit of *Trio Listening and Speaking* is accompanied by a variety of automatically graded activities. Students' progress is recorded, tracked, and fed back to the instructor.

Vocabulary and Grammar Chants help students internalize the target grammar structure and vocabulary for greater accuracy and fluency when listening and speaking.

Vocabulary Oxford 2000 words to talk about exercise and fitness
Put the words in the correct order to make a sentence.

1. practice | to | going | martial | I | am | arts | to | calories | burn | .

2. . | exercise | you | plan | fits | that | your | need | an | schedule

3. attitude | doing | positive | . | yoga | me | gives | a

4. a | good | hike | is | for | going | on | your | heart | .

5. are | ? | to | you | going | basketball | weekend | game | watch | a | this

6. in | works | to | the | shape | he | at | out | gym | . | get

7. me | think | I | gives | . | working | that | energy | out

8. this | ? | going | you | play | are | weekend | to | soccer

Try again Reset Submit

Online Activities provide essential practice of Vocabulary, Grammar, Listening, Speaking, and Pronunication.

GO ONLINE icons lead students to essential digital content.

GO ONLINE for more practice

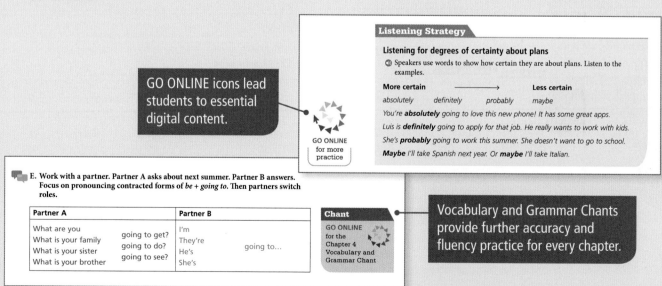

Listening Strategy

Listening for degrees of certainty about plans

Speakers use words to show how certain they are about plans. Listen to the examples.

More certain	——————→		Less certain
absolutely	definitely	probably	maybe

You're **absolutely** going to love this new phone! It has some great apps.

Luis is **definitely** going to apply for that job. He really wants to work with kids.

She's **probably** going to work this summer. She doesn't want to go to school.

Maybe I'll take Spanish next year. Or **maybe** I'll take Italian.

E. Work with a partner. Partner A asks about next summer. Partner B answers. Focus on pronouncing contracted forms of *be + going to*. Then partners switch roles.

Partner A		Partner B	
What are you	going to get?	I'm	
What is your family	going to do?	They're	going to…
What is your sister	going to see?	He's	
What is your brother		She's	

Chant

GO ONLINE for the Chapter 4 Vocabulary and Grammar Chant

Vocabulary and Grammar Chants provide further accuracy and fluency practice for every chapter.

Use the access code on the inside front cover to log in at **www.oxfordlearn.com/login**.

Readiness Unit

Vocabulary

Words and sentences
Verbs
Nouns
Adjectives
Phrases

Listening

Syllable stress
Stress in phrases and sentences
Intonation
Wh- questions
Main ideas and details

Speaking

Syllable and sentence stress
Question intonation
Linking
Reductions
Classroom questions

UNIT WRAP UP ## Extend Your Skills

VOCABULARY

Words and sentences

Words form sentences.

A. Listen to the words and sentences.

Words	Sentences
a, computer, I, need, new	I need a new computer.
a, it's, not, quiet, restaurant	It's not a quiet restaurant.
chair, comfortable, is, the	Is the chair comfortable?
her, is, name, what	What is her name?

Complete sentences have subjects and verbs.

<u>The computer</u> is new.   <u>Ana</u> <u>teaches</u> Spanish.

    subject   verb   subject verb

B. Circle the subject and underline the verb in each sentence.

1. (Cedar Avenue) <u>is</u> a busy street.

2. Lisa is nice.

3. We live downtown.

4. She visits her family every summer.

5. I like this book.

6. Maria studies English.

7. Ken works at the library.

8. I have a new car.

Verbs

English has different parts of speech. Three parts of speech are verbs, nouns, and adjectives.

<u>My family</u> <u>lives</u> in a <u>large</u> <u>apartment</u>.

  noun   verb   adjective noun

The <u>new</u> <u>student</u> <u>rides</u> a <u>red</u> <u>bicycle</u>.

adjective noun   verb adjective noun

Verbs describe actions. They also describe people, things, and feelings. Look at the pictures. Listen to and repeat the sentences.

Actions	People, things, and feelings

Actions

People, things, and feelings

*Marco **plays** soccer.*

*Luis **is** friendly.*

*Lara **speaks** Japanese.*

*We **have** a lot of furniture.*

*We **study** math.*

*I **like** K-pop.*

*Lucas **works** at a museum.*

*She feels **sad**.*

A. Circle the verb in each sentence.

1. I (need) some help.

2. Ana speaks Spanish.

3. Wei has a new bicycle.

4. Marta is busy today.

5. Jun plays basketball on Saturdays.

6. I live in a big apartment building.

7. The teacher is very helpful.

8. I like these shoes.

B. Circle the correct verb to complete each sentence. Then listen and check your answers.

1. I (play) am soccer.

2. My brother lives speaks Spanish.

3. We live have in Chicago.

4. Sophie is has a new bicycle.

5. Ron feels speaks happy today.

6. Dani lives studies music at Cedar College.

7. They like live their new apartment.

8. Tom is has sad today.

Nouns

Nouns describe people, places, and things.

A. Listen and repeat the nouns.

People	Places	Things
Ana	Cedar College	a basketball
Ms. Alvarez	Chicago	a bicycle
my brother	downtown	a book
my friend	San Diego	a class
our family	our street	a job
Sam	the school	art
the teacher	my neighborhood	music

B. Listen to the verbs and nouns. Circle each phrase you hear.

1. speak Spanish   (speak English)

2. work downtown   live downtown

3. love my family   visit my family

4. have a job   do a job

5. like music   like sports

6. is a student   is a teacher

7. play soccer   watch soccer

8. work in San Diego   live in San Diego

C. Circle the noun that goes with each verb.

1. am   *art*   (*a teacher*)

2. speak   *Spanish*   *my neighborhood*

3. live on   *Oak Street*   *a book*

4. visit   *a job*   *Chicago*

5. have   *a car*   *Spanish*

6. need   *downtown*   *help*

7. play   *the city*   *basketball*

8. work at   *pencil*   *the school*

D. Listen and check your answers in Activity C.

E. Use a noun to complete each sentence about yourself. Share your sentences with a partner.

1. I am _____.

2. I speak _____.

3. I have _____.

4. I like _____.

5. I live _____.

6. I study _____.

7. I play _____.

8. I love _____.

Adjectives

🔊 Adjectives describe nouns. Listen to the adjectives and nouns they describe.

People	Places	Things
a **good** teacher	a **busy** street	**expensive** phones
a **friendly** classmate	a **big** store	**old** clothes

🔊 **A. Look at the pictures. Then listen and repeat.**

a *friendly* teacher

a *fun* class

exciting movies

popular music

colorful houses

a *pretty* city

wild animals

a *green* forest

B. Circle the two adjectives that describe the person, place, or thing. Then listen and check your answers.

1. (exciting)   tall   (nice)   music
2. helpful   friendly   red   teacher
3. short   noisy   busy   classroom
4. cheap   happy   useful   phone
5. big   pretty   intelligent   forest
6. friendly   smart   blue   student

C. Put the words in the correct order to form a sentence. Then listen and check your answers.

1. new / Jason / is / a / student

   Jason is a new student.

2. is / Ms. Lee / a / teacher / friendly

   _____

3. live on / a / I / street / quiet

   _____

4. movies / my family / exciting / likes

   _____

5. a / phone / new / has / Mara

   _____

6. drives / Amir / a / car / small

   _____

Phrases

Phrases are groups of words that work together. Two common types of phrases are noun phrases and verb phrases. Listen to the examples.

Noun phrases	Verb phrases
a phone	speak Spanish
nice furniture	have a small car
an exciting movie	live on Oak Street
my teacher	work at the library

A. Listen and circle each noun phrase you hear.

1. (a new computer)   a good computer

2. popular movies   popular music

3. comfortable furniture   comfortable shoes

4. an intelligent student   a busy student

5. a big class   a quiet class

6. a useful phone   a useful book

 **B. Work with a partner. Partner A says a noun phrase in Activity A with *I have,
I want, I like,* or *I am.* Partner B repeats the phrase with *You have, You want,
You like,* or *You are.* Then partners switch roles.**

 C. Listen and circle each verb phrase you hear.

1. live on a quiet street   (live in a big city)

2. work at the museum   visit the museum

3. study art   like art

4. have a small apartment   have a new phone

5. like exciting movies   like exciting TV shows

6. have a nice teacher   have a nice sister

 **D. Work with a partner. Partner A says a verb phrase in Activity C with *I.*
Partner B repeats the phrase with *You.* Then partners switch roles.**

> I live on a quiet street.   You live on a quiet street.

 **E. Put noun phrases and verb phrases together to make sentences. Say the
sentences to your partner. Then switch roles.**

Noun phrases	Verb phrases
my new friend	lives near a beautiful park
Alicia	studies art
the art student	has a small car
the tall girl	rides the bus
my brother	has a nice sister
Ron	likes popular music
the English teacher	plays basketball
Jared	has a big class

Syllable stress

🔊 Some words have one sound called a syllable. Other words have two, three, or more syllables. Usually one or more syllables are louder or stronger. Listen to the examples.

One syllable:	**book**	**chair**	**room**
Two syllables:	**class•room**	**stu•dy**	**teach•er**
Three syllables:	**com•pu•ter**	**di•rec•tions**	**ex•pen•sive**
Four syllables:	**con•ver•sa•tion**	**in•for•ma•tion**	**in•tel•i•gent**

🔊 **A. Listen to each word. Underline the stressed syllable.**

1. <u>friend</u>ly
2. basketball
3. beautiful
4. comfortable
5. apartment
6. exciting
7. busy
8. neighborhood
9. presentation
10. furniture

🔊 **B. Listen to the words in Activity A again. Practice saying the words.**

Stress in phrases and sentences

🔊 Speakers give more stress to certain words in phrases and in sentences. These words are usually verbs, nouns, and adjectives. Speakers don't usually stress small words such as *a*, *an*, *the*, *my*, *some*, *to*, *with*, *in*, *and*, and *at*. Listen to the examples.

a **partner**	**work** with a **partner**	**Work** with a **new partner**.
your **books**	**close** your **books**	**Close** your **English books**.

🔊 **A. Listen and repeat the phrases and sentences.**

1. your **books**	**open** your **books**	**Open** your **books** to **page 3**.
2. the **words**	**repeat** the **words**	**Repeat** the **words** and **phrases**.
3. **groups**	**get** into **groups**	**Get** into **small groups**.
4. the **sentences**	**write** the **sentences**	**Write** the **sentences** on the **board**.
5. the **pictures**	**match** the **pictures**	**Match** the **pictures** and the **words**.
6. your **hand**	**raise** your **hand**	**Raise** your **hand** to **ask** a **question**.
7. a **partner**	**find** a **partner**	**Find** a **new partner**.
8. the **library**	**go** to the **library**	**Go** to the **school library**.

B. Listen. Check (✓) the sentence you hear.

1. ☐ Mr. Lee is a fun teacher. ✓ Mr. Lee is a friendly teacher.

2. ☐ Please work with a new partner. ☐ Please find a new partner.

3 ☐ We need to go to the library. ☐ We need to work at the library.

4. ☐ Open your books and read page 10. ☐ Open your books to page 10.

5. ☐ Work with the same group. ☐ Work with a new group.

6. ☐ Match the pictures and the words. ☐ Look at the pictures and the words.

Intonation

Yes/no questions have rising intonation. The voice goes up (⌣). Statements have falling intonation. The voice goes down (⌢). Listen to the examples.

Question ⌣	Statement ⌢
Are you a new student?	I'm a new student.
Do you play basketball?	I play basketball.
Does your family live in Cedar City?	My family lives in Cedar City.

A. Listen. Check (✓) the question or statement you hear.

Yes/no questions	Statements
1. ✓ Are you in Mr. Lee's class?	☐ You are in Mr. Lee's class.
2. ☐ Are you busy today?	☐ You are busy today.
3. ☐ Do they have a new car?	☐ They have a new car.
4. ☐ Do they live in a big apartment?	☐ They live in a big apartment.
5. ☐ Is your brother a student?	☐ Your brother is a student.
6. ☐ Is the classroom noisy?	☐ The classroom is noisy.
7. ☐ Does your friend like popular music?	☐ Your friend likes popular music.
8. ☐ Does the teacher answer your questions?	☐ The teacher answers your questions.

B. Work with a partner. Partner A says a question or sentence from Activity A. Partner B points to the correct question or statement. Then partners switch roles.

Wh- questions

A. Information questions begin with *wh-* words. Complete the rules about information questions. Then match the examples with the rules.

We use:

1. _____ Who _____ to ask questions about people. __c__
2. _____ to ask questions about things and ideas. _____
3. _____ to ask questions about places. _____
4. _____ to ask questions about time. _____

a. Where is your book?
b. When does class start?
c. ~~Who do you live with?~~
d. What is on your desk?

B. Choose the correct word to complete each sentence. Then listen and check your answers.

1. *Who* (*What*) *Where*   is your name?
2. *Where* *When* *What*   does your family live?
3. *Who* *When* *What*   time is it?
4. *When* *What* *Who*   is your English class?
5. *When* *What* *Who*   is your English teacher this year?
6. *Who* *When* *What*   do you go home?
7. *Where* *Who* *When*   do you study with?
8. *When* *Who* *What*   is your vacation?
9. *When* *What* *Who*   is your favorite color?
10. *Who* *What* *Where*   does your best friend live?

Information questions and sentences usually have falling intonation (⌢↘). Listen to the examples.

⌢↘ What do you study?   ⌢↘ I study English.

⌢↘ Where do you live?   ⌢↘ I live downtown.

⌢↘ Who is your teacher?   ⌢↘ My teacher is Ms. Sanchez.

⌢↘ When is your class?   ⌢↘ My class is at 9 AM.

C. Work with a partner. Partner A asks a question from Activity B. Partner B says a response. Then partners switch roles.

What is your name?   My name is Keiko.

D. Listen to each question. Circle the letter of the correct answer.

1. a. My English teacher is in the classroom.
   (b.) My English teacher is David Valdez.

2. a. I live with my brother.
   b. I live on Oak Street.

3. a. My next class is at 3 PM.
   b. My next class is in the science building.

4. a. That's my phone.
   b. That's my sister.

5. a. I do my homework.
   b. I go to the beach.

6. a. I do my homework at night.
   b. I do my homework at home.

E. Work with a partner to talk about yourself. Partner A asks a question for each answer from Activity D. Partner B answers the question. Then partners switch roles.

> Who is your English teacher?

> My teacher is Jenn.

> Where is your English teacher?

> She's in the classroom.

Main ideas and details

Presentations usually have a main idea. The main idea is the topic of the presentation. Speakers explain the main idea by giving details. Details are examples, explanations, and facts. They help you understand the main idea.

A. Listen to the presentation. Check (✓) the main idea.

☐ things students will learn in their English class

☐ lessons Jim is going to teach the students

☐ activities that help students learn English

B. Listen to the presentation again. What are the students going to do? Check (✓) the details you hear.

☐ watch movies

☐ eat at restaurants

☐ eat at people's homes

☐ play sports at the park

☐ visit places in the area

▲▲▲ SPEAKING

Syllable and sentence stress

Speakers stress certain syllables in words. They also stress certain words—such as verbs, nouns, and adjectives—in sentences.

🔊 A. Listen and repeat the words.

1. ac•**tiv**•i•ty
2. **En**•glish
3. pres•en•**ta**•tion
4. **les**•son
5. **part**•ner
6. **teach**•er
7. in•for•**ma**•tion
8. **an**•swer
9. **nois**•y
10. **li**•brar•y
11. **stu**•dent
12. **friend**•ly

🔊 B. Listen and repeat the phrases and sentences.

1. **studies English**   Sam **studies English**.
2. **have** a **presentation**   We **have** a **presentation**.
3. a **new partner**   I **have** a **new partner**.
4. my **English homework**   This is my **English homework**.
5. the **library**   Sam **studies** at the **library**.
6. a **noisy classroom**   It's a **noisy classroom**.
7. the **answer**   I **know** the **answer**.
8. a **nice teacher**   Mr. **Lee** is a **nice teacher**.
9. a **friendly student**   She's a **friendly student**.
10. a **blue bicycle**   I **have** a **blue bicycle**.

 C. Work with a partner. Partner A says a sentence from Activity B. Partner B points to the correct sentence. Then partners switch roles.

Question intonation

Yes/no questions have rising intonation. Statements and *wh-* questions have falling intonation.

A. Listen and repeat the questions and answers.

Questions	Answers
1. Are you from San Diego? Where is Sue from?	No, I'm not. I'm from LA. She's from Toronto.
2. Is this the English class? When does class start?	Yes, it is. It's English 101. It starts at 9 AM.
3. Is the teacher helpful? What does he do?	Yes, he is. He's a helpful teacher. He answers our questions.
4. Is Ana your friend? What does she like?	Yes, Ana is my friend. She likes exciting movies.
5. Are you good at sports? What is your favorite sport?	Yes, I'm good at sports. My favorite sport is basketball.
6. Do you know Jake and Amy? Where do they live?	Yes, I know them. They live in my neighborhood.

 B. Work with a partner. Practice the questions and answers in Activity A.

Linking

Linking is connecting sounds in words. Speakers often connect the last sound in a word with the first sound in the next word. For example, speakers often link consonants with vowels. Listen to the example.

I live in a big apartment. We have a lot of furniture.

Note: *t* sometimes sounds like *d* before a vowel.

A. Listen and repeat.

1. work at the museum   I work at the museum.

2. has a new bicycle   Wei has a new bicycle.

3. is a student   Ana is a student.

4. live in San Diego   I live in San Diego.

5. have a job   You have a job.

6. an intelligent student   Is he an intelligent student?

7. kind of music   I like this kind of music.

8. an exciting movie   We saw an exciting movie.

B. Listen and repeat the questions and answers. Pay attention to the linked sounds.

1. Where do you live?   I live on Cedar Street.
2. Where does she work?   She works at the library.
3. What does he have?   He has a new bicycle.
4. What is it like?   It's an expensive car.
5. What do you do?   I study English at Cedar College.

C. Work with a partner. Ask and answer the questions in Activity B. Pay attention to the linked sounds.

Reductions

 People sometimes speak quickly and reduce sounds. For example, speakers often reduce *of.* It sounds like "a." Listen to the examples.

kind of → *kinda*   *some of* → *soma*   *most of* → *mosta*   *a lot of* → *a lotta*

A. Listen and repeat.

1. What do you read?   I read a lot of books.
2. What kind of movies do you like?   I like exciting movies.
3. What's the problem?   Some of the words are hard.
4. Do you like English?   Yes. It's kind of easy.
5. How's your class?   Great! Most of the students are really nice.
6. Are some of the students here?   They're all here.

B. Work with a partner. Ask and answer the questions in Activity A. Pay attention to the reduced sounds.

> What do you read?   I read a lot of books.

Classroom questions

 Students often ask questions in class. Sometimes they want to hear something again. Sometimes they need an explanation of something. Sometimes they want other help. Speakers make these questions polite by adding *Excuse me* and *please*. Listen to the examples.

Excuse me.   *Can you repeat that please?*

                    What does…mean?

A. Listen and repeat.

Requests for repetition and clarification	Other requests
What did you say?	What is that?
Did you say...?	Can you help me please?
Can you repeat that please?	How do you spell...?
Can you say that again please?	How do you pronounce...?
What do you mean by...?	Where's the stress in...?
What does that mean?	How do you stress...?

B. Circle the best answer for each question. Then listen and check your answers.

1. A: Can you help me please?
   B: I said, "Open you books to page 8."
   B: Sure. What do you need?

2. A: What does that mean?
   B: M - E - A - N.
   B: It means "very smart."

3. A: Excuse me. What does *huge* mean?
   B: Sure. Open your books to page 8.
   B: It means "very big."

4. A: Excuse me. How do you spell *huge*?
   B: H - U - G - E.
   B: You stress the first syllable.

5. A: Excuse me. Where's the stress in *activity*?
   B: You stress the second syllable.
   B: A - C - T - I - V - I - T - Y.

6. A: Excuse me. What is that word?
   B: Sure. Work with a new partner.
   B: It's a noun.

7. A: What does *difficult* mean?
   B: It means "not easy."
   B: You stress the first syllable.

8. A: What is that?
   B: Sure. I said, "See you tomorrow."
   B: It's a notebook.

C. Work with a partner. Ask and answer the questions in Activity A.

Can you help me please?

Sure. What do you need?

D. Complete the conversations with the words from the box. Then listen and check your answers.

| again | ~~excuse~~ | mean | repeat | spell | stress |

1. A: So, is everyone ready? OK. Please open your books to page 14. Yes, Jun?

   B: _____Excuse_____ me. Did you say page 40?

   A: No, I said page 14.

   B: OK. Thanks.

2. A: Ms. Lee?

   B: Yes, Ana?

   A: Can you help me please?

   B: Sure.

   A: How do you _____ *intelligent*?

   B: It's I - N - T - E - L - L - I - G - E - N - T.

   A: Thank you!

3. A: Now, please find a new partner. Practice the words with your partner. Yes, Yoshi?

   B: Umm, excuse me. Where is the _____ in this word?

   A: Oh, presentation. It's on the third syllable.

   B: Thanks.

4. A: Is it *pre-**sen**-ta-tion*?

   B: No. _____ the word: *pre-sen-**ta**-tion*.

   A: *Pre-sen-**ta**-tion*.

   B: Good!

   A: Thank you.

5. A: Excuse me.

   B: Yes, Marco.

   A: What does *repetition* _____?

   B: It means saying something again.

   A: Oh, thank you.

6. A: Next, match the pictures and the words.

   B: I'm sorry. Can you say that _____?

   A: Sure. I said, "Match the pictures and the words."

   B: Thanks.

E. Practice the conversations in Activity D with a partner.

Look at the word bank for the Readiness Unit. Check (✓) the words you know. Circle the words you want to learn better.

OXFORD 2000 🔑

Adjectives		Nouns		Verbs	
beautiful	happy	activity	information	answer	open
big	hard	apartment	job	do	play
blue	helpful	art	library	eat	repeat
busy	intelligent	board	movie	feel	say
cheap	nice	book	museum	find	see
easy	noisy	bus	music	get	speak
exciting	old	car	night	go	spell
expensive	popular	chair	park	have	stress
favorite	pretty	class	partner	help	study
friendly	red	clothes	phone	know	visit
fun	short	college	phrase	live	watch
good	tall	computer	picture	match	work
green	wild	conversation	question	mean	write
		family	sentence	need	
		furniture	show		
		group	street		
		hand			

PRACTICE WITH THE OXFORD 2000 🔑

A. Use the chart. Match adjectives with nouns.

1. _beautiful clothes_   2. _____

3. _____   4. _____

5. _____   6. _____

B. Use the chart. Match verbs with nouns.

1. _repeat the word_   2. _____

3. _____   4. _____

5. _____   6. _____

C. Use the chart. Match verbs with adjective noun partners.

1. _find a cheap apartment_   2. _____

3. _____   4. _____

5. _____   6. _____

UNIT 1 Science and Technology

CHAPTER **1** ## How Are You Preparing for Your Future?

▲ **VOCABULARY**
- Oxford 2000 🔑 words to talk about plans for the future

▲▲ **LISTENING**
- Listening for reasons
- Listening for examples

▲▲▲ **SPEAKING**
- Linking *wh-* question words with *is/are*
- Reporting on plans for the future

CHAPTER **2** ## How Will You Get Around?

▲ **VOCABULARY**
- Oxford 2000 🔑 words to talk about transportation of the future

▲▲ **LISTENING**
- Listening for disagreement
- Listening for numerical information

▲▲▲ **SPEAKING**
- Linking *will* in information questions
- Predicting the future of transportation

CHAPTER **3** ## What Does It Do?

▲ **VOCABULARY**
- Oxford 2000 🔑 words to talk about new technologies

▲▲ **LISTENING**
- Listening for similarities and differences
- Listening for topic shift

▲▲▲ **SPEAKING**
- Linking third person *-s* endings with articles and nouns
- Describing a favorite new technology

UNIT WRAP UP ## Extend Your Skills

CHAPTER 1

How Are You Preparing for Your Future?

- Use the present progressive
- Listen for reasons
- Recognize *-ing* in the present progressive

- Listen for examples
- Link *wh-* question words with *is/are*
- Report on plans for the future

▲ VOCABULARY ▶ Oxford 2000 ✏ words to talk about plans for the future

Learn Words

🔊 **A. Label each picture with the correct word(s). Then listen and repeat the words and phrases.**

| business   a career   college   computer science   design   job experience   ~~music~~   problems |

1.

major in _____music_____

2.

study _____

3.

solve _____

4.

take _____

5.

graduate from _____

6.

plan _____

7.

go into _____

8.

get _____

The present progressive

🔊 Speakers use the present progressive to describe actions that are happening right now. Speakers usually use contractions in the present progressive. Listen to the examples.

> **I am** majoring in art. → **I'm** majoring in art.
>
> **She is** studying engineering. → **She's** studying engineering.
>
> They **are not** taking math classes. → They **aren't** taking math classes.

🔊 To ask questions, speakers use *am/is/are* before the subject. Listen to the examples.

> A: **Are** you **majoring** in math?   B: No, I'm not.
>
> A: What **is** she **studying**?   B: She's studying music.

🔊 **B. Listen and repeat.**

1. Are you learning Japanese?   No, I'm learning Spanish.
2. Is he studying business?   No, he's studying law.
3. Are they teaching music?   No, they're teaching design.
4. Are you going to City College?   No, I'm going to Cedar College.
5. What is she taking?   She's taking a design course.
6. Who are you working with?   I'm working with Alicia.
7. What are they majoring in?   They're majoring in computer science.
8. Who are you talking to?   I'm talking to you.

💬 **C. Work with a partner. Ask and answer the questions in Activity B.**

🔊 **D. Listen and check (✓) the sentence you hear.**

1. [✓] She's studying English.   [ ] She studies English.
2. [ ] He's working at the library.   [ ] He works at the library.
3. [ ] They aren't listening to music. [ ] They don't listen to music.
4. [ ] We're going to Cedar College.   [ ] We go to Cedar College.
5. [ ] Is she teaching computer science here?   [ ] Does she teach computer science here?
6. [ ] Who are you talking to?   [ ] Who do you talk to?

💬 **E. Work with a partner. Partner A says a sentence from Activity D. Partner B points to the correct sentence. Then partners switch roles.**

Learn Phrases

🔊 **A. Match each phrase to the correct picture. Then listen and repeat.**

a job that **pays well**	have **a job I love**
be **comfortable with** technology	have good **people skills**
do **something creative**	prepare for a **career in medicine**
good at **solving problems**	interested in **the music business**

1.

2.

3.

4.

5.

6.

7.

8.

B. Listen to each conversation. Check (✓) the phrase you hear.

1. ☐ a job that pays well   ✓ comfortable with technology

2. ☐ do something creative   ☐ good at solving problems

3. ☐ have good people skills   ☐ have a job I love

4. ☐ a job that pays well   ☐ have a job I like

5. ☐ preparing for a career in medicine   ☐ a job that pays well

6. ☐ interested in the music business   ☐ do something creative

C. Add job words to complete the sentences.

A lawyer A(n) _____ banker _____	has a job that pays well.
A painter A(n) _____	has a job that is creative.
A teacher A(n) _____	has good people skills.
A nurse A(n) _____	has a career in medicine.
A musician A(n) _____	has a job in the music business.

D. Work with a partner. Ask and answer the questions.

Partner A	Partner B
1. What are you good at? 3. Do you enjoy helping people? 5. Is making a lot of money important to you?	2. What do you enjoy doing? 4. What are you studying in school? 6. What are you planning to do in the future?

What are you good at?

I'm really good at math.

GO ONLINE
for more
practice

CONVERSATION

🔊 **A. Listen to the conversation. What are Ana, Samir, and Rob talking about? Check (✓) the topics you hear.**

☐ classes	☐ jobs	☐ majors
☐ teachers	☐ vacations	

🔊 **B. Listen to the conversation again. Match the classes from the box with the students.**

art	computer science	math	music	science

1. Ana's taking _____ and _____ classes.

2. Samir's taking _____ classes.

3. Rob's taking _____ and _____ classes.

Listening Strategy

Listening for reasons

🔊 Speakers use certain words to connect activities with reasons. Listen to the examples.

            activity   **reason**
Why am I studying fashion? **Because** *I love clothes.*

                reason   **activity**
Tomás wants to design buildings, **so** *he's majoring in architecture.*

           reason   **activity**
I'm good with kids. **That's why** *I want to be a teacher.*

GO ONLINE
for more
practice

🔊 **C. Listen to part of Ana, Samir, and Rob's conversation again. Match each activity with the reason.**

Activity

1. Ana is majoring in computer science.
_____

2. Samir is majoring in biology. _____

3. Rob wants to do something with art. _____

Reason

a. He or she wants a career in medicine.

b. He or she thinks it's fun.

c. He or she is comfortable with technology.

Reduction of *-ing* with the present progressive

When speakers use the present progressive, the *-ing* verb ending sometimes sounds like *n*. Listen to the examples.

I'm **taking** art classes. → I'm **takin** art classes.

What are you **studying**? → What are you **studyin?**

D. Listen to the speakers. Check (✓) the sentence you hear.

1. ☐ They're taking a lot of music classes. ✓ They're takin a lot of music classes.

2. ☐ She's planning a career in medicine. ☐ She's plannin a career in medicine.

3. ☐ We're studying at Cedar College this year. ☐ We're studyin at Cedar College this year.

4. ☐ Is he playing soccer or basketball this year? ☐ Is he playin soccer or basketball this year?

5. ☐ What are you working on right now? ☐ What are you workin on right now?

6. ☐ Where are you going after class? ☐ Where are you goin after class?

E. Work with a partner. Partner A says a sentence from Activity D. Partner B points to the correct sentence. Then partners switch roles.

F. Listen to the questions. Complete each question with the word you hear.

1. What are you _____watching_____ on TV these days?

2. What are you _____ today?

3. How are you _____ right now?

4. What books are you _____ this semester?

5. What are you _____ about right now?

G. Work with a partner. Ask and answer the questions in Activity F. Practice making the present progressive verb end in *n*.

What are you watching on TV these days?

I'm watching a lot of sports. What about you?

Chant

GO ONLINE for the Chapter 1 Vocabulary and Grammar Chant

A. Look at the list of subjects. Think about jobs you can have if you like these subjects. Write your ideas in the chart.

Subjects	Jobs
computer science	
math	
music	
art/design	
business	

 B. Work in a group of three. Compare your answers in Activity A and answer the questions.

1. Were your job ideas the same or different?

2. Did you learn about any new jobs for each subject? What are they?

C. Listen to the first part of the presentation. What is the speaker talking about? Circle the correct answer.

types of jobs   *things you can buy*   *good places to work*

D. Listen to the entire presentation. Answer the questions.

1. What was Tom's major?

_____

2. What does Tom design today?

_____

3. What does Claudia build?

_____

4. What did Yoshi major in?

_____

5. What kind of people does Yoshi help?

_____

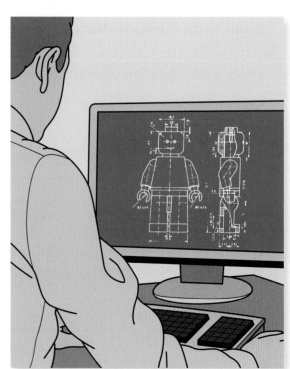

Listening for examples

GO ONLINE
for more
practice

Speakers give examples to help listeners understand their main ideas. Phrases such as *for example* and *for instance* introduce examples. Listen to the examples.

> *Good communication skills are important in most jobs.*
>
> **For example**, *it's important to have good speaking skills in business.*
>
> **For instance**, *scientists write a lot.*

 E. Listen to part of the presentation again. The speaker uses students as examples. Match the students with the ideas.

| Claudia | Tom | Yoshi |

1. _____ You can work as web developer or in the information technology department of a big company. But you can also work in design.

2. _____ You can build bridges and highways. But you can also work in space exploration.

3. _____ There are also STEM careers in music.

F. Work with a partner. Ask and answer the questions.

Partner A	Partner B
1. What are STEM careers?	2. What are two good things about STEM jobs?
3. What kinds of majors prepare people for STEM careers?	4. What does the speaker think about STEM careers?
5. What is an example of a STEM job that isn't boring?	6. What are some more examples about STEM?

Discuss the Ideas

 G. Work in a group. Discuss your answers to the questions.

1. Were you surprised by the information about STEM careers? Why or why not?

2. Do you know anyone who has a STEM career? What does the person do? Where does he or she work?

3. Do you want to have a STEM career? Why or why not?

▲▲▲ SPEAKING

Speaking Task Reporting on plans for the future

Step 1 PREPARE

Pronunciation Skill

Linking *wh-* question words with *is/are*

🔊 When speakers ask *wh-* questions in the present progressive, they often link the final consonant sound in the *wh-* word with the vowel sound at the beginning of *is* and *are*. Listen to the examples.

Notice that *t* sounds like *d* before a vowel sound.

What is he studying? → **Whadiz** he studying?

When are you leaving? → **Whener** you leaving?

Where are they going? → **Wherer** they going?

How is she doing? → **Howiz** she doing?

Why are you taking math? → **Whyer** you taking math?

GO ONLINE
for more
practice

🔊 **A. Listen and repeat.**

1. What	What are	What are you listening to?
2. When	When is	When is he coming?
3. Where	Where are	Where are you working?
4. What	What is	What is she doing?
5. How	How are	How are you getting there?
6. Where	Where is	Where is she studying?
7. What	What are	What are you wearing?
8. Who	Who are	Who are you talking to?

 B. Work with a partner. Partner A asks a question from Activity A. Partner B points to the question. Then partners switch roles.

C. Listen. Complete each conversation with the words you hear.

are you going	are you majoring	~~are you planning~~	are you preparing	are you studying	are you taking

1. A: What _____ are you planning _____ to do after you graduate?

   B: I'm going to travel.

2. A: What _____?

   B: French and music.

3. A: Where _____ right now?

   B: Home.

4. A: Why _____ in computer science?

   B: Because I'm good at solving problems.

5. A: Why _____ music classes?

   B: I want to be a music teacher.

6. A: Why _____ for a STEM career?

   B: Because there are a lot of interesting STEM jobs, and they pay well, too.

GO ONLINE to practice the conversations

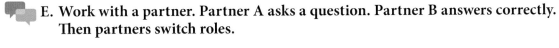 **D. Work with a partner. Practice the conversations in Activity C.**

E. Work with a partner. Partner A asks a question. Partner B answers correctly. Then partners switch roles.

A	B
1. a. What are you listening to these days?	A lot of K-pop.
b. Where are you listening to music these days?	In my car.
2. a. How are you learning Portuguese?	I want to visit Brazil.
b. Why are you learning Portuguese?	I'm taking an online course.
3. a. What is Kim doing today?	She's playing soccer.
b. How is Kim doing today?	She's doing great.
4. a. When are you going downtown?	Ali.
b. Who are you going downtown with?	This afternoon.
5. a. How is your brother getting to school?	At 8 AM.
b. When is your brother getting to school?	He's driving.
6. a. Why is Keith studying engineering?	At the University of San Diego.
b. Where is Keith studying engineering?	He wants to build robots.

A. **Think about yourself. What are you good at? What do you enjoy doing? What are you thinking of doing in the future? Complete the chart.**

I'm good at...	I like...	In the future, I might...

 B. **Work with a partner. Talk about the things you're good at, what you like to do, and what you might do in the future. Use your notes in Activity A.**

Speaking Skill

Giving reasons

Speakers use *because* and *so* to give reasons for their ideas, feelings, activities, and plans. Listen to the examples.

Because introduces a reason:

           plan   reason
I want to do something with art **because** *it's fun for me.*

So and *that's why* follow a reason:

        reason   activity
I'm good with kids, **so** *I'm planning a career in education.*

        reason   plan
I love to travel. **That's why** *I'm going to take a trip right after graduation.*

Word Partners

a successful career

a long career

a professional career

career goals

career planning

career opportunities

GO ONLINE
to practice
word partners

C. **Complete the sentences about you. Use the ideas in the chart in Activity A or new ideas.**

1. I'm good at _____. That's why _____.
2. I enjoy _____, so _____.
3. I want/don't want to have my own business because _____.
4. I like/don't like solving problems. That's why _____.
5. I am/am not good with people, so I probably _____.
6. Making a lot of money is/isn't important to me, so _____.
7. I'm studying _____ because I want to _____.
8. I'm thinking about a career in _____ because _____.

 D. **Compare your ideas in Activity C with a partner.**

Speaking Task

Reporting on plans for the future

1. Work with a partner. Find out about your partner's plans for the future, the reasons for these plans, and what your partner is doing to prepare for these plans. Use the questions in the chart or your own questions.

Name: _____	
Questions	**Answers**
1. What are you thinking about doing in the future?	
2. Why?	
3. What are you doing to prepare?	

2. Practice asking and answering the questions in the chart with a partner.

3. Work in a small group. Close your books. Tell your group about your partner's plans. Then listen to your group members' plans and ask questions.

Step 3 REPORT

A. Think about the information you heard about your classmates. Write a detail you remember about three classmates.

Classmate	Detail

Step 4 REFLECT

Checklist

Check (✓) the things you learned in Chapter 1.

○ I learned language for talking about the future.

○ I used language for giving reasons.

○ I reported on a classmate's plans for the future.

Discussion Question

Do you think you will change your mind about your plans for the future? Why or why not?

CHAPTER **2** How Will You Get Around?

- Use *will/won't*
- Listen for disagreement
- Recognize contractions with *will* and *won't*

- Listen for numerical information
- Link *will* in information questions
- Predict the future of transportation

▲ VOCABULARY ► Oxford 2000 🔑 words to talk about transportation of the future

Learn Words

A. Label each picture with the correct word(s). Then listen and repeat the words and phrases.

accident	car	distances	free time	public transportation	road	town	traffic

1.

have ___free time___

2.

pay attention to the _____

3.

travel long _____

4.

use _____

5.

buy a self-driving _____

6.

cause a(n) _____

7.

avoid _____

8.
get around _____

Grammar Note

will/won't

Speakers use *will/won't* + verb to talk about facts in the future or to make predictions (say what they think will happen in the future). Listen to the examples.

Traffic **will get** worse in the future.   prediction: I think this will happen.

I **won't drive** to school tomorrow.   fact: I know this will happen.

To make questions, put *will* before the subject. Listen to the examples.

Will you **buy** a new car? No, I **won't**.

How **will** Sam **get** to school? He**'ll take** the subway.

B. Listen and repeat.

1. I'll take the train.

2. It'll be warm tomorrow.

3. She'll like it.

4. You won't be late.

5. They won't avoid traffic.

6. Will it be expensive?

7. Where will he be next year?

8. When will we get there?

C. Listen and repeat each question and answer.

1. Will you buy a new car soon?   No, I won't. I don't have enough money.

2. Will traffic in this city get worse or better?   It'll get worse. There are too many cars on the road.

3. Will you study English next year?   Yes, I will. I'll take English 200.

4. What will happen after you graduate?   I'll get a job and save some money.

5. How will people travel long distances in the future?   They'll take high-speed trains.

6. What will the weather be like tomorrow?   It'll rain. I heard the weather report.

D. Work with a partner. Ask the questions in Activity C. Give answers that are true for you.

Learn Phrases

A. Match each phrase to the correct picture. Then listen and repeat.

having your own car is **more private**	make it easier for **older people**
a lot of cars **on the road**	cars that drive themselves **have a lot of benefits**
change the way we **travel long distances**	cars that **communicate with each other**
get around in the future	cars are **expensive to operate**

1.

2.

3.

4.

5.

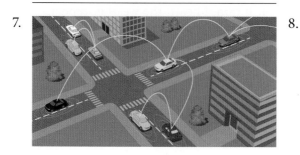

6.

7.

8.

B. Listen to each conversation. Check (✓) the phrase you hear.

1. ☐ have a lot of benefits ✓ make it easier for older people

2. ☐ change the way we travel long distances ☐ a lot of cars on the road

3. ☐ change the way we travel long distances ☐ cars that drive themselves have a lot of benefits

4. ☐ cars are expensive to operate ☐ use technology to communicate with each other

5. ☐ have a lot of benefits ☐ having your own car is more private

6. ☐ make it easier for older people ☐ get around in the future

C. Read each question. Circle your answer or give your own.

1. How do you get around town?

   I take public transportation.   I drive my own car.   I _____.

2. Why do you do that?

   It's more private.   It isn't expensive.   It _____.

3. How will you get around in the future?

   I'll have a car that drives itself.   I'll take public transportation.   I'll _____.

4. Why will you do that?

   It won't be expensive.   It will be easier for an older person.   It will _____.

D. Work with a partner. Take turns asking and answering the questions in Activity C.

How do you get around town?

I ride my bike.

Really? Why do you do that?

It's good exercise, and it isn't expensive like a car.

GO ONLINE
for more
practice

▲▲ LISTENING

CONVERSATION

🔊 **A. Listen to the conversation. What is it about? Circle the correct answer.**

avoiding traffic   *having accidents*   *a type of car*

🔊 **B. Listen to the conversation again. Circle the correct word(s) to complete each sentence.**

1. Luis   *doesn't want*   *wants*   to control the car.

2. Self-driving cars will make the roads   *more*   *less*   dangerous.

3. Self-driving cars can   *avoid*   *cause*   accidents.

4. With self-driving cars, people   *will*   *won't*   have to pay attention to the road.

Listening Strategy

Listening for disagreement

🔊 Speakers use certain expressions to show the other person that they disagree. They often soften their disagreement by saying *I don't know* or *I'm not sure.* Listen to the examples.

> A: There are a lot of good things about living downtown.
>
> B: I'm not sure I agree.
> B: I don't know about that.
> B: I'm not sure about that.
> B: I don't think so.

GO ONLINE
for more practice

🔊 **C. Listen to parts of the conversation again. Circle the expression you hear.**

1. Kaylee: Aren't cars that drive themselves great?

   Luis: Oh, you mean self-driving cars?   *No. I don't think so.*   *I'm not sure I agree.*

2. Kaylee: Computers control them, not people. Computers are smarter than people.

   Luis: *I don't know about that.*   *I'm not sure about that.*

3. Kaylee: Right. That causes accidents. With self-driving cars, people won't have to pay attention, so there'll be fewer accidents.

   Luis: Hmm...   *I don't know about that.*   *I'm not sure about that.*

 D. Work with a partner. Partner A says a statement. Partner B uses an expression from the Listening Strategy box to disagree. Then partners switch roles.

Cars that drive themselves are great.

Cars that drive themselves are dangerous.

Cars that drive themselves have a lot of benefits.

Cars are expensive to operate.

Contractions with *will* and *won't*

Speakers usually use contractions with *will*. They contract the subject and *will* in the affirmative. They contract *will* and *not* in the negative. Listen to the examples.

I will see you tomorrow. → *I'll* see you tomorrow.

It will save you some money. → *It'll* save you some money.

He will be there next week. → *He'll* be there next week.

She *will not* come with us. → She *won't* come with us.

You *will not* like this. → You *won't* like this.

They *will not* graduate this year. → They *won't* graduate this year.

E. Listen and repeat the sentences in the Sounds of English box.

F. Listen and circle the sentence you hear.

1. It will rain tomorrow.   It'll rain tomorrow.

2. They will have more free time.   They'll have more free time.

3. He will take the subway.   He'll take the subway.

4. We will not take the train to LA. We won't take the train to LA.

5. She will not have an accident.   She won't have an accident.

6. You will not avoid traffic.   You won't avoid traffic.

G. Listen to each conversation. Write the contraction you hear.

1. A: Will he buy a new car?

   B: No, he _____ won't _____.

2. A: How will you get to school?

   B: _____ take the bus.

3. A: Where will the new subway line go?

   B: _____ go to the airport.

4. A: Will they take a vacation this year?

   B: No, they _____.

5. A: When will she start driving?

   B: _____ start when she's 16.

6. A: When will he graduate?

   B: _____ graduate next spring.

H. Work with a partner. Practice the conversations in Activity G.

> **Chant**
>
> GO ONLINE for the Chapter 2 Vocabulary and Grammar Chant

A. Think about cars and other types of transportation such as buses and trains. Write your ideas in the chart.

	A car	Public transportation
Is it inexpensive or expensive to operate or use?		
Is it fast or slow?		
Is it private?		
Are you in control?		
What are some other good things about it?		
What are some other problems with it?		

B. Compare your ideas in Activity A with a partner.

C. Listen to the introduction. Complete the sentence.

The transportation experts are going to talk about transportation _____.

D. Listen to the entire panel discussion. Write the details in the box in the correct places in the chart.

give you more free time	the Hyperloop	inexpensive	more freedom than the bus	self-driving cars

Speaker	Form of transportation	Benefits
Sylvie Ng	_____	_____ fewer accidents on the road
David Martinez	_____	fast _____
Grant Rich	personal transportation pod	_____ more privacy than the bus

Listening for numerical information

Speakers often use facts in predictions. Facts include numbers such as times (years, dates) and amounts (time, money, people, things). Listen to the examples.

Times	**Amounts**
I will graduate from Cedar College **by next June**.	*Cedar College will have* **1,000** *math majors next year.*
In 2050, *most people will take public transportation.*	*In the future, you will fly to Japan in* **three hours**.
By 2050, *most people will not own a car.*	*A small car will cost more than* **$100,000**.

GO ONLINE
for more
practice

E. Listen to each prediction from the panel discussion. Write the numerical information you hear. Then listen again and check your answers.

1. By _____, we'll start to see self-driving cars on the road.

2. By _____, there will be _____ million self-driving cars on the road.

3. By _____, almost all cars will be self-driving.

4. Air pushes each compartment through the tube at _____ miles per hour.

5. People will be able to go from San Francisco to Los Angeles in _____ minutes.

6. And tickets may cost only $_____ per passenger.

F. Listen to the panel discussion again. Then ask and answer the questions with a partner.

Partner A	Partner B
1. What are the experts talking about?	2. What does the Hyperloop look like?
3. What are some things people can do in self-driving cars?	4. When will we start seeing self-driving cars on the road?
5. How does the Hyperloop work?	6. Where are people using personal transportation pods right now?

Discuss the Ideas

G. Work with a partner. Practice asking and answering the questions.

1. Which type of transportation in the panel discussion is the most certain?

2. Which type of transportation in the panel discussion is the most useful in your opinion? Why?

▲▲▲ SPEAKING

Speaking Task Predicting the future of transportation

Step 1 PREPARE

Pronunciation Skill

Linking *will* in information questions

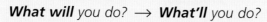 Speakers usually link question words such as *what, where,* and *when* with *will.* They link the final sound of the question word with the contracted form of *will.* Listen to the examples.

> ***What will** you do?* → ***What'll** you do?*
>
> ***Where will** he go?* → ***Where'll** he go?*
>
> ***When will** they get here?* → ***When'll** they get here?*
>
> ***Who will** be there?* → ***Who'll** be there?*

GO ONLINE
for more
practice

A. Listen to the questions. Check (✓) *same* **if you hear the same question. Check (✓)** *different* **if the questions are different.**

1. [✓] same   [ ] different

2. [ ] same   [ ] different

3. [ ] same   [ ] different

4. [ ] same   [ ] different

5. [ ] same   [ ] different

6. [ ] same   [ ] different

B. Listen and repeat.

1. How   How'll   How'll you get there?

2. When   When'll   When'll it start?

3. Who   Who'll   Who'll be there?

4. Where   Where'll   Where'll you buy it?

5. What   What'll   What'll you study?

6. When   When'll   When'll it be here?

C. Listen. Complete the conversation with the contracted forms of the words in the box. Responses may be used more than once.

how will	what will	where will

Wei: I'm thinking about buying a car.

Mari: Wow! Cars are expensive. _____How'll_____ you pay for everything?

Wei: Well, I actually have the money right now. I saved it working part time.

Mari: Fantastic! So, _____ you get?

Wei: I'm thinking about getting one of those small electric cars—a plug-in car.

Mari: Those are so cute! _____ you plug it in to charge it?

Wei: There's a charging station right next to my apartment building.

Mari: So, next question: _____ you buy this great-sounding car?

Wei: Well, that's the problem. There's no dealership around here. I have to go into the city.

Mari: _____ you get there?

Wei: Can you borrow your brother's car and drive me there?

Mari: Sure. I'd love to come with you.

GO ONLINE
to practice the conversation

D. Work with a partner. Practice the conversation in Activity C.

E. Work with a partner. Partner A asks a question. Partner B answers correctly. Then partners switch roles.

1. a. Where'll the Hyperloop go?   Like a tube.
   b. What'll it look like?   It'll go from San Francisco to LA.

2. a. What'll it cost to go from San Francisco to LA?   About $20.
   b. What'll people like about the Hyperloop?   It's fast.

3. a. What'll people like about personal transportation pods?   They're private.
   b. When'll they be available?   They're available in a few places right now.

4. a. Who'll want a self-driving car?   Read, watch TV, or do work.
   b. What'll people do in a self-driving car?   People who don't like driving.

5. a. Who'll have a self-driving car in the future?   They'll communicate with each other.
   b. How'll self-driving cars avoid accidents?   Almost everyone.

Step 2 SPEAK

A. List at least three types of transportation in the chart. Then list two benefits for each one.

Types of transportation	Benefits
____________	1. ____________ 2. ____________
____________	1. ____________ 2. ____________
____________	1. ____________ 2. ____________

B. Work with a partner. Compare your charts from Activity A.

Word Partners

take public transportation, a train, a bus, a plane

go by public transportation, car, train, bus, plane

get on/off a train, a bus, a plane

ride a bicycle

GO ONLINE to practice word partners

Speaking Skill

Using future time markers in predictions

Speakers use future time expressions in predictions to show the time they are talking about. Listen to the examples.

Someday, *people will live in space.*

In the future, *everyone will speak the same language.*

Sometime in the future, *there will be fast trains between San Francisco and Los Angeles.*

By 2050, *I will have my own business.*

C. Make predictions about the future. Use the ideas in the box or your own ideas. Tell your predictions to a partner. Then switch roles.

have self-driving cars have flying cars travel from New York to London in one hour travel in space live on Mars	Someday, ... In the future, ... Sometime in the future, ... By [year], ...

Speaking Task

Predicting the future of transportation

1. Prepare for your presentation. How will people get around in the future? Write predictions in the chart.

What type of transportation is it?	
What will it look like?	
How will it work?	
What benefits will it have?	
When will this happen?	

2. Practice making your predictions with a partner.

3. Work in a group. Close your books. Tell your group about your predictions. Give as much information as you can. Listen to your group members' predictions and ask questions.

Step 3 REPORT

A. Review your group members' predictions. Write notes in the chart.

1. Which type of transportation has the most benefits?	
2. Which type of transportation will people like the most? Why?	

B. Share your notes with the class. Which prediction do you think will happen? Why?

Step 4 REFLECT

Checklist

Check (✓) the things you learned in Chapter 2.

○ I learned language for talking about the future.

○ I recognized disagreement.

○ I made a prediction about the future of transportation.

Discussion Question

Why do we need to think of new ways to get around?

- Use the third person singular
- Listen for similarities and differences
- Recognize /s/, /z/, and /iz/ for third person singular
- Listen for topic shift
- Link third person singular -s endings with articles and nouns
- Describe a favorite new technology

▲ VOCABULARY ▶ Oxford 2000 ⚷ words to talk about new technologies

Learn Words

A. Label each picture with the correct words. Then listen and repeat the phrases.

comes in	connects to	keeps track of	~~plays~~	makes	stores	takes	tells

1.

___plays___ music and

_____ pictures

2.

_____ the time and

_____ social media

3.

_____ steps and calories and

_____ information

4.

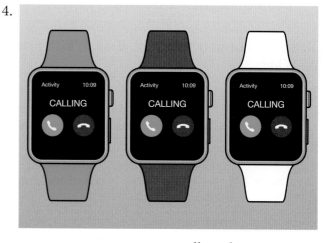

_____ calls and

_____ different colors

Grammar Note

Third person singular

Speakers use the simple present tense to talk about facts and actions that occur regularly. The third person singular in the simple present tense ends with an -s. Use *does* with the base form of the verb to ask questions. Listen to the examples.

Does he **study** engineering? → *Yes, he does. He* **studies** *engineering at Cedar College.*

Where **does** *she* **work**? → *She* **works** *at the school.*

What **does** *it* **do**? → *It* **washes** *windows.*

B. Listen and check (✓) the form you hear.

1. [✓] I take pictures.   [ ] It takes pictures.

2. [ ] I record my steps.   [ ] It records my steps.

3. [ ] I talk to people.   [ ] It talks to people.

4. [ ] They build robots.   [ ] She builds robots.

5. [ ] They connect to apps.   [ ] It connects to apps.

6. [ ] They avoid traffic.   [ ] He avoids traffic.

C. Work with a partner. Partner A says a sentence from Activity B. Partner B points to the correct sentence. Then partners switch roles.

D. Complete each sentence with the simple present tense form of the verb in parentheses. Then listen and check your answers.

1. What does that phone do?   (play) It _____plays_____ music.

2. What does that app do?   (record) It _____ my steps.

3. What does that watch do?   (connect) It _____ to my laptop.

4. What does that robot do?   (clean) It _____ the floor.

5. What does that car do?   (avoid) It _____ traffic.

6. What does that computer do?   (control) It _____ the car.

E. Work with a partner. Ask and answer the questions in Activity D.

Learn Phrases

A. Match each phrase to the correct picture. Then listen and repeat.

a camera that's **fun and easy to use**	get the **latest technological devices**
a watch that **comes with a fitness app**	robot that **looks like a person**
does jobs that are **dangerous or boring**	talks and **recognizes faces**
does jobs **around the house**	understands and **shows emotions**

1.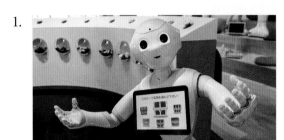

2.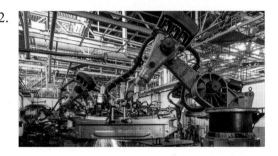

3.

4.

5.

6.

7.

8.

B. Listen to the speakers. Circle the best answer for each question.

1. What is the woman talking about? *a camera*   *a robot*

2. What is the speaker talking about? *a person*   *a robot*

3. What kinds of things might the man see at the show? *toys*   *computers*

4. Where will they be this afternoon? *outdoors*   *at home*

5. Where does Baxter work? *in a factory*   *at home*

6. What app does the woman like best? *the fitness app*   *the music app*

 C. Work with a partner. Ask and answer the questions.

1. What are some jobs that are dangerous or boring?

2. What are some jobs you do around the house?

3. What apps did your phone come with?

4. What are some technological devices that aren't fun and easy to use?

5. Do you usually get the latest technological devices, or do you wait to buy them?

6. What do you think about robots that look like people?

> What are some jobs that are dangerous or boring?

> Cleaning the house is boring.

D. Work with a partner. Partner A uses a phrase to describe a device. Partner B guesses the device. Then partners switch roles.

Partner A		Partner B	
It	keeps track of steps.	It's	an app.
	does dangerous jobs.		a camera.
	does jobs around the house.		a phone.
	recognizes faces.		a robot.
	takes pictures.		a watch.
	tells the time.		

GO ONLINE for more practice

CONVERSATION

🔊 **A. Listen to the conversation. What are the speakers talking about? Circle the correct answer.**

phones   *watches*   *computers*

🔊 **B. Listen to the conversation again. Check (✓) the facts and actions that the speakers talk about.**

☐ records steps _____   ☐ makes calls _____

☐ keeps track of calories _____   ☐ connects to apps _____

☐ plays music _____   ☐ tells the time _____

☐ stores information _____   ☐ comes in different colors _____

Listening Strategy

Listening for similarities and differences

🔊 Speakers use expressions to describe similarities and differences. Listen to the examples.

Similarities	Differences
It's **the same**.	It's **not the same**.
It's **similar**.	It's **different**.
My phone does that, **too**.	It **isn't like** that.

GO ONLINE for more practice

🔊 **C. Listen to parts of the conversation again. Complete the sentences with the words you hear.**

1. Jun: This one comes in eight colors. What about yours?
   Sara: My watch is _____.

2. Sara: It records my steps. What about yours?
   Jun: Mine is _____.

3. Jun: It keeps track of how many calories I burn, too.
   Sara: My watch _____.

D. How is Jun's watch different from Sara's watch? Write *J* for *Jun* and *S* for *Sara* next to the facts and actions you checked in Activity B.

/s/, /z/, and /iz/ for third person singular

The third person singular -s ending in the simple present tense has three sounds.
Listen to the examples.

Sounds like /s/	Sounds like /z/	Sounds like /iz/
hits	avoids	fixes
laughs	goes	judges
stops	saves	washes
walks	sings	watches

E. Listen and repeat.

1. walk   walks   He walks to school.

2. stop   stops   It stops at red lights.

3. teach   teaches   She teaches music.

4. send   sends   It sends messages.

5. fix   fixes   He fixes dinner.

6. save   saves   It saves money.

F. Work with a partner. Use the words in the chart and your own ideas to ask and answer questions.

Question		Answer	
What does that...do?	watch	It	stores information.
	tablet		plays music.
	laptop		keeps track of steps.
	phone		makes calls.
	app		tells the time.
	device		connects to apps.
What does your...do?	sister	He	works at the school.
	brother	She	teaches math.
	mother		fixes cars.
	father		designs robots.
	aunt		studies engineering.
	uncle		takes art classes.
	friend		

Chant

GO ONLINE
for the
Chapter 3
Vocabulary and
Grammar Chant

A. Work with a partner. Discuss your answers to the questions.

What do you see in each picture? What do you think each thing does?

B. Listen to the first section of the talk. Check (✓) the best definition of a *service robot.*

☐ a machine that does jobs that are too dangerous or difficult for people to do

☐ a machine that does jobs around the house and takes care of people

☐ a machine that does work that people do not want to do

Listening Strategy

Listening for topic shift

Speakers use expressions to tell the audience that they are moving to the next topic. Listen to the examples.

Now, **let's move on** *to...*

The next thing *I'm going to discuss is...*

Let's take a look at...

GO ONLINE
for more
practice

C. Listen to the whole talk. Number the topics in the correct order.

_____ a more advanced service robot

_____ simple service robots

_____ a human-like service robot

D. Listen to the talk again. Complete the mind map with the details from the box. You will use one detail twice.

cleans the floor	cuts grass
dances	expresses emotions
~~gets people up~~	gives weather reports
plays games	reminds people of appointments
talks	washes windows

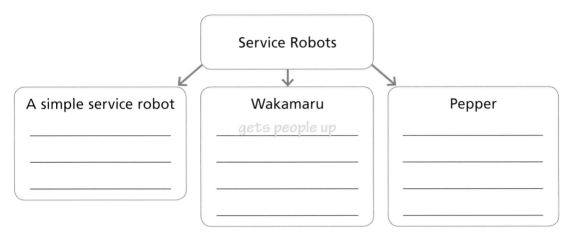

Service Robots

A simple service robot
_____
_____
_____

Wakamaru
gets people up
_____
_____
_____

Pepper
_____
_____
_____

E. Listen to the talk again. Then ask and answer the questions with a partner.

Partner A	Partner B
1. What is the definition of a *robot*?	2. How is a service robot different from other types of robots?
3. What does the first type of service robot do?	4. What language does Wakamaru speak?
5. How is Pepper different from Wakamaru?	6. What does the company that made Pepper predict?

Discuss the Ideas

F. Work with a partner. Discuss your answers to the questions.

1. What are possible benefits of service robots? What are possible problems with service robots?

2. Some service robots take care of children or disabled people. Is this a good thing or a bad thing? Explain your answer.

3. Would you like a household robot? Why or why not?

Speaking Task Describing a favorite new technology

Step 1 PREPARE

Pronunciation Skill

Linking third person singular -s endings with articles and nouns

◀)) When using the simple present tense, speakers link the final -s sound with the beginning vowel sound of the word that follows it. Listen to the examples.

He teaches a music class. → *He teach**iza** music class.*

It avoids accidents. → *It avoid**za**ccidents.*

She takes a train. → *She take**sa** train.*

◀)) **A. Listen and repeat.**

1. a career	has a career	She has a career in medicine.
2. information	records information	It records information.
3. apps	runs apps	It runs apps for exercising.
4. a break	takes a break	He takes a break at noon.
5. emotions	shows emotions	It shows emotions, too.
6. appliances	fixes appliances	It fixes appliances.

◀)) **B. Listen and check (✓) the sentence you hear.**

1. ☐ The robots run apps.   ✓ She has a career in medicine.

2. ☐ My friends watch a movie on Saturdays.   ☐ It records information.

3. ☐ The students take English online.   ☐ It runs apps for exercising.

4. ☐ The website gives a weather report.   ☐ He takes a break at noon.

5. ☐ The factory makes a new kind of car.   ☐ It shows emotions, too.

6. ☐ The engineers design appliances.   ☐ The engineer designs appliances.

GO ONLINE for more practice

C. Work with a partner. Partner A says a sentence from Activity B. Partner B points to the correct sentence. Then partners switch roles.

D. Listen. Complete each conversation with a phrase from the box.

comes in five colors	~~runs exercise apps~~
does a lot of things	takes a yoga
fixes electric cars	teaches an art

1. A: Why do you like that watch?

   B: Because it _____ runs exercise apps _____ .

2. A: So, what is Randi doing these days?

   B: She _____ class.

3. A: What does Wakamaru do?

   B: It _____ .

4. A: Which phone do you recommend?

   B: I like this one because it _____ .

5. A: What does Yulia do on Saturday?

   B: She _____ class.

6. A: What does your mechanic do?

   B: He _____ .

GO ONLINE
to practice the
conversations

 E. Work with a partner. Practice the conversations in Activity D.

A. Look at the list of technological devices and add your own ideas. Which do you know about? Which do you have? Which do you want to have? Check (✓) the ones you have. Write *W* for *want* and/or *K* for *know about* for the others.

Technological devices	What does it do?
☐ the latest smartphone _____	
☐ a tablet _____	
☐ the latest laptop _____	
☐ a smart watch _____	
☐ a self-driving car _____	
☐ a service robot _____	
☐ a human-like robot _____	
☐ the latest video camera _____	
☐ a smart refrigerator _____	
☐ _____	
☐ _____	

Word Partners

modern technology

advanced technology

current technology

new technology

the latest technology

GO ONLINE
to practice
word partners

 B. Work with a partner. Look at the chart in Activity A. For each device you know about, write something it does in the second column.

Speaking Skill

Presenting additional information

Speakers use certain expressions to add information when they are describing something. Listen to the examples.

*Pepper the Robot speaks Japanese. It **also** understands emotions. It shows them, **too**. **Another thing** Pepper can do is dance.*

 C. Choose one of the devices in Activity A and describe it to your partner. Talk about what it does. Add information with the expressions in the Word Partners box.

A smart refrigerator keeps track of the food inside it. It also tells you when you need to buy more food. It controls the temperature, too.

Speaking Task

Describing a favorite new technology

1. What is your favorite new technology? Make notes about it in the chart.

Device	How does it work? What does it do?	Why do you like it?

2. Use your notes to describe your technology to a partner.

3. Work in a small group. Close your books. Tell your group about your favorite new technology. Then listen to your group members' descriptions and ask questions.

Step 3 REPORT

A. Choose the most interesting technology that a group member described. Work with a new small group. Tell your group about the technology you chose. Complete the notes to describe what it does and give a reason to explain why it's interesting.

My classmate's favorite new technology is the _____. It

_____. It also _____. It

_____, too. I think it's the most interesting new technology

because _____.

B. List the new technologies that you heard about in your groups. Then vote for the most interesting one.

Step 4 REFLECT

Checklist

Check (✓) the things you learned in Chapter 3.

○ I learned language for talking about facts and actions.

○ I understood people comparing technology.

○ I described a favorite technological device and reported on a classmate's favorite device.

Discussion Question

Why do technological devices such as phones change so often?

Look at the word bank for Unit 1. Check (✓) the words you know. Circle the words you want to learn better.

OXFORD 2000 ⚷

Adjectives	Nouns		Verbs	
boring	accident	house	come	pay
comfortable	benefit	job	communicate	play
dangerous	business	medicine	connect	recognize
easy	car	music	get	show
expensive	career	people	have	solve
fun	college	problem	keep	store
long	computer	road	look	take
old	design	science	love	tell
own	device	skill	make	travel
private	distance	town	operate	use
public	emotion	traffic		
	experience	transportation		
	face			

PRACTICE WITH THE OXFORD 2000 ⚷

A. Use the chart. Match adjectives with nouns.

1. _____expensive devices_____   2. _____

3. _____   4. _____

5. _____   6. _____

B. Use the chart. Match verbs with nouns.

1. _____get around town_____   2. _____

3. _____   4. _____

5. _____   6. _____

C. Use the chart. Match verbs with adjective noun partners.

1. _____use public transportation_____   2. _____

3. _____   4. _____

5. _____   6. _____

UNIT 2 Health and Wellness

CHAPTER **4** **How Are You Going to Get in Shape?**

△ **VOCABULARY**
- Oxford 2000 ⚷ words to talk about exercise and fitnesss

△△ **LISTENING**
- Listening for degrees of certainty about plans
- Distinguishing facts from opinions

△△△ **SPEAKING**
- Practicing reductions with *going to, want to, have to,* and *need to*
- Describing a fitness plan

CHAPTER **5** **Can We Work as a Team?**

△ **VOCABULARY**
- Oxford 2000 ⚷ words to talk about teamwork

△△ **LISTENING**
- Listening for past time markers in a story
- Listening for explanations

△△△ **SPEAKING**
- Practicing verbs with *-ed* endings
- Describing a team experience

CHAPTER **6** **What Was It Like?**

△ **VOCABULARY**
- Oxford 2000 ⚷ words to talk about healthy environments

△△ **LISTENING**
- Listening for ways speakers show interest and understanding
- Listening for problems and solutions

△△△ **SPEAKING**
- Linking *was/wasn't/were/weren't* with vowels
- Describing how a change made life better, safer, or healthier

UNIT WRAP UP **Extend Your Skills**

CHAPTER 4

How Are You Going to Get in Shape?

- Use *be + going to*
- Listen for degrees of certainty about plans
- Recognize the contraction of *be + going to*

- Distinguish facts from opinions
- Practice reductions with *going to,* *want to, have to,* and *need to*
- Describe a fitness plan

▲ VOCABULARY ► Oxford 2000 🔑 words to talk about exercise and fitness

Learn Words

🔊 **A. Label each picture with the correct words. Then listen and repeat the phrases.**

do	go	go on	play	~~practice~~	ride	watch	work out

1.

_____practice_____ martial arts and

_____ yoga

2.

_____ soccer and

_____ a basketball game

3.

_____ swimming and

_____ at the gym

4.

_____ a hike and

_____ a bike

Grammar Note

be + going to

Speakers use *be + going to* to talk about future plans. The simple form of the verb follows *going to*. Speakers usually contract the subject and *be* in the affirmative. Listen to the example.

> **I'm going to** walk to school tomorrow, Marisol **is going to** take the bus, and Tim and Amir **are going to** drive their car.

To ask questions, use *be* before the subject. Listen to the examples.

> **Is** he **going to buy** a new car this year?

> How **is** she **going to get** to the station?

> **Are** you **going to study** English next year?

> Where **are** you **going to buy** your new phone?

B. Listen and repeat.

1. going to do
2. going to go
3. going to play
4. going to ride
5. going to watch
6. going to work out

C. Listen to each conversation. Circle the answer you hear.

1. Are you going to do yoga at the gym?
   - *Yes, I am. There's a class at noon.*
   - *No, I'm not. I'm going practice martial arts.*

2. Are you going to play basketball this weekend?
   - *Yes, I am. I'm going to play with Jen and Caitlin.*
   - *No, I'm not. I'm going to watch a soccer game on TV.*

3. Are we going to ride our bikes this weekend?
   - *Yes, we are. We're going to ride to the beach.*
   - *No, we're not. We're going to work out at the gym.*

4. Is Rob going to go to school this summer?
   - *Yes, he is. He's going to take an art class.*
   - *No, he isn't. He's going to visit friends in Mexico.*

5. Are you going to buy a car someday?
   - *Yes, I am. I'm going to get a self-driving car.*
   - *No, I'm not. They're too expensive.*

6. Are you going to take a vacation this year?
   - *Yes, I am. I'm going to visit my family.*
   - *No, I'm not. I'm going to stay home and work.*

 D. Work with a partner. Ask and answer the questions in Activity C.

Learn Phrases

A. Match each phrase to the correct picture. Then listen and repeat.

doing martial arts helps you **get in shape**	exercising **gives you energy**
running helps you **burn calories**	make an exercise plan that **fits your schedule**
doing yoga **gives you a positive attitude**	it's **good for your heart**

1.

2.

3.

4.

5.

6.

B. Listen to each conversation. Circle the correct answer.

1. The man thinks that exercising   *burns calories.*   *gives you energy.*

2. The man does martial arts to   *stay in shape.*   *give him a positive attitude.*

3. The woman thinks that working out helps   *burn calories.*   *give you a positive attitude.*

4. The woman thinks that exercising   *gives you energy.*   *gives you a positive attitude.*

5. The doctor thinks think that exercising   *burns calories.*   *is good for the heart.*

6. The man thinks the woman needs an exercise plan   *that fits her schedule.*   *to give her a positive attitude.*

 C. Work with a partner. Ask and answer the questions. Use the bold phrases in your questions and answers.

1. What activity gives you **a positive attitude?**

2. What is the best way to **burn calories?**

3. What activity **gives you energy?**

4. What are some ways to **get in shape?**

> What activity gives you a positive attitude?

> Running always gives me a positive attitude. What about you?

D. Work with a partner. Partner A completes the sentence about exercise plans. Partner B completes the sentence about exercise benefits. Then partners switch roles.

Partner A		Partner B	
I'm going to	do yoga.	Great! You're going to	burn calories.
	do martial arts.		get in shape.
	exercise at lunchtime.		have a healthy heart.
	play basketball.		keep a positive attitude.
	work out at the gym.		make an exercise plan that fits your schedule.

GO ONLINE for more practice

CONVERSATION

🔊 **A. Listen to the conversation. Who is going to be more active this weekend? Circle the correct name.**

Mariko   *Andy*

🔊 **B. Listen to the conversation again. What activities are Mariko and Andy going to do this weekend? Check (✓) the correct answers.**

☐ watch TV   ☐ get some sleep

☐ go swimming   ☐ take a martial arts class

☐ take an exam   ☐ go on a bike ride

☐ study for an exam   ☐ go on a hike

Listening Strategy

Listening for degrees of certainty about plans

🔊 Speakers use words to show how certain they are about plans. Listen to the examples.

More certain ⟶ **Less certain**

absolutely   definitely   probably   maybe

*You're **absolutely** going to love this new phone! It has some great apps.*

*Luis is **definitely** going to apply for that job. He really wants to work with kids.*

*She's **probably** going to work this summer. She doesn't want to go to school.*

***Maybe** I'll take Spanish next year. Or **maybe** I'll take Italian.*

GO ONLINE
for more
practice

🔊 **C. Listen to parts of the conversation again. Complete the sentences with the words in the box. Responses may be used more than once.**

absolutely	definitely	maybe	probably

1. Andy: I'm _____probably_____ going to hang around my apartment.

2. Andy: What about you? Are you going to relax?

   Mariko: _____ not! I'm going to get some fresh air and exercise.

3. Mariko: Yep. I'm _____ going to take a martial arts class on Saturday, then I'm going to go on a long bike ride.

4. Mariko: And _____ I'll go swimming on Sunday.

5. Andy: Well, I don't know about you, but I'm _____ going to feel better by Monday morning. I'm staying right here on the couch.

Contraction of *be* + *going to*

Speakers usually use contractions with *be* + *going to*. They contract the subject and *be* in the affirmative. They contract *be* with *not* in the negative. Listen to the examples.

I am going to ride my bike. → **I'm** going to ride my bike.

She is going to graduate next year. → **She's** going to graduate next year.

We are going to take the subway. → **We're** going to take the subway.

D. Listen and check (✓) the phrase you hear.

1. [✓] they are going to go   [ ] they're going to go

2. [ ] he is going to come   [ ] he's going to come

3. [ ] she is going to get   [ ] she's going to get

4. [ ] I am going to see   [ ] I'm going to see

5. [ ] he is going to take   [ ] he's going to take

6. [ ] we are going to play   [ ] we're going to play

E. Work with a partner. Partner A asks about next summer. Partner B answers. Focus on pronouncing contracted forms of *be* + *going to*. Then partners switch roles.

Partner A		Partner B	
What are you What is your family What is your sister What is your brother	going to get? going to do? going to see?	I'm They're He's She's	going to...

Chant

GO ONLINE for the Chapter 4 Vocabulary and Grammar Chant

A. Check (✓) the reasons people exercise. Add your own ideas. Share your ideas with a partner.

☐ for fun

☐ to lose weight

☐ to get strong

☐ to relax

☐ _____

☐ _____

B. Listen to the first section of the show. Circle the topic of the show.

the benefits of exercise   *different types of exercise*   *exercise mistakes*

C. Listen to the first and second sections of the show. Circle the correct answer to each question.

1. Does exercise help you lose weight?   *It helps you a little bit.*   *It doesn't help you at all.*

2. What happens when people exercise? They burn calories at   *the end of*   *the beginning of*   an exercise program.

3. How do we know this?   *Researchers   Lucia Suarez*   did a study at City University of New York.

4. The research shows that you might lose weight when you   *start   stop*   an exercise program.

Listening Strategy

Distinguishing facts from opinions

A fact is something that a person can prove, for example, with an experiment. An opinion is an idea. No one proved it, but someone might prove it in the future. Speakers use *prove, show,* and *find* to introduce a fact. They use *think* and *believe* to introduce an opinion. Listen to the examples.

*Some people **think** exercise helps you lose weight.*	This is just an idea.
*However, a study **showed** that exercise does not always burn calories.*	A study proved this.

GO ONLINE
for more
practice

D. Listen to the third section of the show. Complete each sentence with the word you hear.

believe   show   showed   think

1. Most experts _____ that <u>exercise has a lot of emotional benefits.</u>

                                         F   O

2. Some studies _____ that <u>people felt happier and more relaxed when</u> <u>they exercised regularly.</u>

                                         F   O

3. Many studies _____ that <u>exercise is good for your heart.</u>

                                         F   O

4. Some experts also _____ that <u>people who exercise don't get sick as</u> <u>often as people who don't exercise.</u>

                                         F   O

E. Work with a partner. Are the underlined ideas in Activity D facts or opinions? Circle *F* for *fact* or *O* for *opinion.*

F. Listen to the show again. Ask and answer the questions with a partner.

Partner A	Partner B
1. Does exercising always help you lose weight? 3. When does exercising help you lose weight? 5. What is one benefit of exercising?	2. Who did a study about exercising and weight loss? 4. What is the best way to make an exercise plan? 6. What is another benefit of exercising?

Discuss the Ideas

G. What are some reasons people don't exercise? Check (✓) the problems and add your own idea.

☐ They don't have time.

☐ It costs too much money.

☐ It doesn't help them lose weight.

☐ It hurts.

☐ It's boring.

☐ _____

H. Work with a partner. Think of solutions for the problems in Activity G.

SPEAKING

Speaking Task Describing a fitness plan

Step 1 PREPARE

Pronunciation Skill

Reduction of *going to, want to, have to,* and *need to*

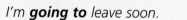 Speakers often combine and shorten verb phrases with *to* such as *going to, want to, have to,* and *need to.* Listen to the examples.

I'm **going to** leave soon. →	I'm **gonna** leave soon.
Do you **want to** go with us? →	Do you **wanna** go with us?
I **have to** see this. →	I **hafta** see this.
What do you **need to** do? →	What do you **needta** do?

GO ONLINE
for more practice

A. Listen and check (✓) the sentence you hear.

1. [✓] We're going to get some sleep.   [ ] We're gonna get some sleep.

2. [ ] I have to get some fresh air.   [ ] I hafta get some fresh air.

3. [ ] When do you want to go swimming?   [ ] When do you wanna go swimming?

4. [ ] They want to lose some weight.   [ ] They wanna lose some weight.

5. [ ] He's going to fall asleep on the couch.   [ ] He's gonna fall asleep on the couch.

6. [ ] Do you need to buy a new car?   [ ] Do you needta buy a new car?

B. Listen and repeat the questions and answers.

1. What are you going to do this weekend?   I'm going to work out at the gym.

2. When do you want to take a vacation?   We want to take a vacation next spring.

3. Where do you want to go?   We want to go to San Diego.

4. What do you have to do this evening?   I have to do chores around the house.

5. Where do you have to go tomorrow?   I have to go downtown.

6. What do you need to do before an exam?   I need to read the textbook.

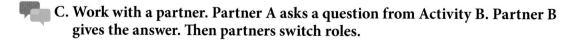 **C. Work with a partner. Partner A asks a question from Activity B. Partner B gives the answer. Then partners switch roles.**

D. Listen. Complete the conversation with the phrases you hear. Responses may be used more than once.

going to	have to	need to	want to

A: So, Miles, what are you _____ *going to* _____ do this summer?

B: I'm _____ get a job.

A: A job?

B: Yeah, I _____ make some money so I can buy a new car.

A: So, what kind of job do you _____ get?

B: I _____ find a job that pays well.

A: That makes sense.

B: And we worked out all year at the gym, so I _____ keep fit, too.

A: Good idea. So, what kind of job do you think you'll find?

B: My uncle owns a gym. I'm _____ ask him for job.

A: Fantastic! So you can work out and make money at the same time.

B: That's the idea. So, what about you? What are you _____ do this summer?

A: Same here. I _____ keep fit, too, so I'm _____ get a job at the pool.

B: Sounds like we'll both be in good shape next fall.

GO ONLINE to practice the conversation

 E. Work with a partner. Practice the conversation in Activity D.

A. Some people want to get in shape outside of a gym. What are some interesting ways to do this? Write your ideas in the first column in the chart.

Ways to keep fit	Who will this work for?	Benefits (Why will this work?)

B. Who will your fitness ideas work for? Think about different groups of people such as students, workers, parents, and so on. Write your ideas in the middle column in the chart in Activity A.

C. Work with a partner. Think of three benefits for each way to get in shape in the chart in Activity A. Add your ideas to the third column.

Word Partners

be fit

get fit

keep fit

look fit

stay fit

GO ONLINE
to practice
word partners

Speaking Skill

Describing benefits

When speakers describe a plan, they explain how the plan will benefit people. They show the good things about the plan. Speakers use examples and reasons to explain benefits. Listen to the examples.

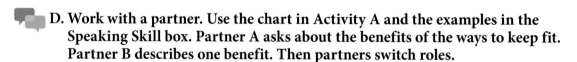

Our fitness plan has many benefits. For example, **it will work for busy people** *because* **it only takes 15 minutes a day.** **It's also inexpensive** *because* **people don't need any special equipment with our plan.**

D. Work with a partner. Use the chart in Activity A and the examples in the Speaking Skill box. Partner A asks about the benefits of the ways to keep fit. Partner B describes one benefit. Then partners switch roles.

Partner A		Partner B
How will...benefit	students? workers? parents?	It will benefit...because...

Speaking Task

Describing a fitness plan

1. Look at your notes in Step 2. Choose one way to keep fit. Explain how it will work and who it's for. Make a list of benefits. Organize your ideas in the chart.

My fitness plan	Who is this for?	Benefits

2. Close your book. Work in a group. Describe your plan to your group. Ask your group members questions about their plans.

Step 3 REPORT

A. Write sentences about your group members' plans. Then discuss what plan will work the best and why.

Name	Plan description	Benefits

 B. Work with a new partner. Describe the plan you want to try. Why do you want to try it?

Step 4 REFLECT

Checklist

Check (✓) the things you learned in Chapter 4.

○ I learned language to describe a fitness plan.

○ I understood a conversation about exercise plans.

○ I described a fitness plan for a particular group of people.

Discussion Question

What are some other ways to stay healthy, especially for students?

CHAPTER 5 Can We Work as a Team?

- Use simple past regular and irregular verbs
- Listen for past time markers in a story
- Recognize the contraction of *didn't*
- Listen for explanations
- Practice verbs with *-ed* endings
- Describe a team experience

▲ VOCABULARY ▶ Oxford 2000 ♪ words to talk about teamwork

Learn Words

◉ **A. Label each picture with the correct words. Then listen and repeat the phrases.**

| achieve | have | learn | play | support | take on | win | work |

1.

_____play_____ on a team and

_____ a game

2.

_____ a challenge and

_____ a goal

3.

_____ as a team and

_____ a lesson

4.

_____ each other and

_____ success

Grammar Note

Simple past regular and irregular verbs

Speakers use the simple past to describe actions that were completed in the past. To form the simple past, add *-ed* to regular verbs. For irregular verbs, memorize the simple past forms. Listen to the examples.

I **study** art at Cedar College. → I **studied** art at Cedar College last year.

He **works** in the music business. → He **worked** in the music business in 2015.

To ask questions, speakers use *did* before the subject. Listen to the examples.

A: **Did** she **design** robots?   B: No, she didn't. She **designed** toys.

A: How **did** they **get** there?   B: They **took** public transportation.

B. Listen and check (✓) the statement you hear.

1. ☐ We play soccer on Saturday.   ☑ We played soccer on Saturday.

2. ☐ They study music at Cedar College.   ☐ They studied music at Cedar College.

3. ☐ I don't work at the gym.   ☐ I didn't work at the gym.

4. ☐ They stay home in the evening.   ☐ They stayed home in the evening.

5. ☐ You like your math classes.   ☐ You liked your math classes.

6. ☐ We don't watch the game on TV.   ☐ We didn't watch the game on TV.

C. Listen to each question. Circle the answer you hear.

1. Did you play basketball in high school?   (Yes, I did. It was fun.)
   No, I didn't. I played soccer.

2. Did you win a lot of games?   Yes, we did. We won every game.
   No, we didn't. We weren't very good.

3. Did you buy an electric car?   Yes, I did. It wasn't too expensive.
   No, I didn't. I bought a regular car.

4. Where did you work last summer?   I worked at a gym.
   I worked at the school.

5. Why did your team succeed?   We supported each other.
   We worked hard.

 D. Work with a partner. Ask and answer the questions in Activity C.

Learn Phrases

🔊 **A. Match each phrase to the correct picture. Then listen and repeat.**

a team can **get the job done faster**	students on teams **get better grades**
each person **sees things in a different way**	teamwork is **the key to success**
put people **into teams**	**work together** to solve a problem

1.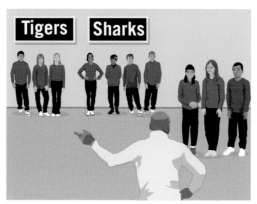

2.

3.

4.

5.

6.

B. Listen to the conversations. Match the phrases with the situations.

a. a team can get the job done faster

b. each person sees things in a different way

c. put people into teams

d. ~~team players have a positive image of themselves~~

e. teamwork is the key to success

f. work together to solve a problem

Situation 1: ___d___

Situation 2: _____

Situation 3: _____

Situation 4: _____

Situation 5: _____

Situation 6: _____

C. Work with a partner. Ask and answer the questions. Use the bold phrases in your questions and answers.

1. What kind of jobs can you **get done faster** as a team?

2. Do you know someone who **has a positive image of himself or herself**? Describe this person.

3. What is **the key to success at school**, in your opinion?

4. What are some current issues that **people see in different ways**?

What kind of jobs can you get done faster as a team?

Cleaning the house. What do you think?

Moving furniture.

GO ONLINE
for more
practice

▲▲ LISTENING

CONVERSATION

◉ **A. Listen to Emma's story. What is she talking about? Circle the correct answer.**

how to play basketball   *how to work as a team*   *how to support classmates*

◉ **B. Listen to the story again. What does *teamwork* mean? Check (✓) the correct answers.**

☐ Team members support each other.

☐ Each team member is stronger than the team.

☐ Team members have a good attitude about themselves.

☐ Team members have their own goals.

☐ Team members work together.

Listening Strategy

Listening for past time markers in a story

◉ Speakers use expressions to refer to specific times in the past such as *last summer, during that year, the next year, when...,* and *in 2015*. Listen to the examples.

When *I was a child, my family and I lived in Spain for 12 months. I learned a lot* **during that year**.

In 2015, *we got a new volleyball coach.* **The next year**, *we started to win games.*

GO ONLINE
for more
practice

◉ **C. Listen and complete the sentences with the correct time expressions from the box.**

at the beginning	during that year	in 2015	the next year	that year	when

1. I was on the soccer team _____.

2. I played baseball _____ of the year.

3. We learned a lot about teamwork _____.

4. _____ I was in college, I moved to the United States.

5. _____, we got a new teacher.

6. We traveled a lot _____.

Sounds of English

Contraction of *didn't*

🔊 Speakers usually use a contraction for *did + not*. Listen to the examples.

I **did not** play volleyball in school. → I **didn't** play volleyball in school.

She **did not** graduate last year. → She **didn't** graduate last year.

They **did not** watch the game last night. → They **didn't** watch the game last night.

🔊 **D. Listen and check (✓) the statement you hear.**

1. ✓ Ana did not major in computer science. ☐ Ana didn't major in computer science.

2. ☐ We did not see a lot of cars on the road. ☐ We didn't see a lot of cars on the road.

3. ☐ Luis did not get a STEM job. ☐ Luis didn't get a STEM job.

4. ☐ The robots did not communicate with each other. ☐ The robots didn't communicate with each other.

5. ☐ The team members did not achieve their goal. ☐ The team members didn't achieve their goal.

6. ☐ The phone did not come with a fitness app. ☐ The phone didn't come with a fitness app.

🔊 **E. Complete each conversation with the contracted form of *did + not* or *did + not* + verb. Then listen and check your answers.**

1. A: Did you watch the basketball game last night?
   B: No, I _____. I missed it.

2. A: Sophie played volleyball in high school, right?
   B: No, she _____ volleyball. She played soccer.

3. A: Did you like the lecture on robots?
   B: Actually, I _____ it. It was too complicated.

4. A: How was the new high-speed train?
   B: Super fast. We got there in 30 minutes. I _____ time to read my book.

5. A: Why _____ the project succeed?
   B: Because they _____ as a team.

Chant

GO ONLINE for the Chapter 5 Vocabulary and Grammar Chant

A. In what situations do you work cooperatively with other people? Check (✓) the situations and add your own ideas. Then think of examples of working cooperatively in these situations.

☐ at home ☐ in sports

☐ at school ☐ _____

☐ at work ☐ _____

B. Work as a group to discuss your ideas in Activity A. Share your ideas with the class.

C. Listen to the introduction. Where are the speakers? Circle the correct answer.

in a gym   *in a class*   *in a business office*

D. Listen to the rest of the lecture. What are the benefits of teamwork according to the lecture? Check (✓) the ideas you hear.

People who work in teams…

☐ have better attitudes. ☐ are more creative.

☐ have better physical health. ☐ have better communication skills.

☐ get more work done.

Listening Strategy

Listening for explanations

Speakers often explain key ideas. They state a main idea and then give an explanation of it. This helps them give a more complete picture of their ideas. Listen to the examples.

idea	explanation

A lot of students are preparing for STEM careers. Science, technology, engineering, and math courses are very popular this year.

idea	explanation

Robots do jobs that are dangerous or boring. They do jobs that people don't want to do such as building things in factories.

idea	explanation

Personal transportation pods give people a lot of freedom. With pods, people can go where they want to go when they want.

GO ONLINE
for more
practice

E. Listen to parts of the lecture again. Match the explanations to the main ideas.

Main Ideas	Explanations
1. _____ A team can get more work done than one person can.	a. People who work in teams often feel better about themselves.
2. _____ People are more creative when they work together.	b. Different people can work on different parts of a project and get them done faster.
3. _____ Teamwork has emotional benefits.	c. Each person on the team can see things in a different way.

F. Listen to the main part of the lecture again. Circle the letter of the best phrase to complete each statement.

1. The architecture students showed that _____.

   a. people are more creative when they work together

   b. a team can get more work done than one person can

2. The phone company team showed that _____.

   a. people are more creative when they work together

   b. teamwork has emotional benefits

3. The study on high school students showed _____.

   a. that teamwork has emotional benefits

   b. people are more creative when they work together

G. Listen to the lecture again. Then ask and answer the questions with a partner.

Partner A	Partner B
1. What class are the students taking?	2. Besides sports, where is teamwork important?
3. What are the benefits of teamwork?	4. What did the architecture team do?
5. What did the phone company team do?	6. What did the study show about students who play on sports teams?

Discuss the Ideas

H. Work in small groups. Discuss your answers to the questions. Then report your ideas to the class.

1. Do you like to work on teams? Why or why not?

2. Think of a time when a team didn't work well. What was the situation? Why didn't it work?

▲▲▲ SPEAKING

Speaking Task Describing a team experience

Step 1 PREPARE

Pronunciation Skill

Verbs with *-ed* endings

🔊 Simple past tense endings with *-ed* have three sounds. Listen to the examples.

Sounds like /t/	Sounds like /d/	Sounds like /id/
stopped	*achieved*	*avoided*
talked	*designed*	*supported*
watched	*learned*	*texted*
worked	*played*	*waited*

GO ONLINE
for more
practice

🔊 **A. Listen and repeat.**

1. walk	walked	We walked home.
2. achieve	achieved	I achieved my goal.
3. text	texted	He texted me.
4. play	played	They played soccer.
5. start	started	She started working out.
6. improve	improved	It improved my attitude.
7. work	worked	The plan worked.

🔊 **B. Listen. Check (✓) the sentence you hear.**

1. ✓ I work on Saturday.   ☐ I worked on Saturday.

2. ☐ They graduate this year.   ☐ They graduated this year.

3. ☐ We save a lot of money.   ☐ We saved a lot of money.

4. ☐ You stop the car here.   ☐ You stopped the car here.

5. ☐ I play soccer at school.   ☐ I played soccer at school.

6. ☐ We avoid accidents.   ☐ We avoided accidents.

78 Unit 2 | Chapter 5

C. Listen. Complete the conversation with the words from the box.

asked	connected	decided	designed	~~enjoyed~~	improved
liked	posted	showed	talked	worked	

Carla: Aren't you glad the semester is over? I'm going to relax and have fun this summer!

Jun: I actually _____ *enjoyed* _____ school this year.

Carla: Really? What did you like about it?

Jun: I really _____ a team project we did in Mr. Conner's class.

Carla: What did you do?

Jun: We _____ online with another English class. They were in

Atlanta. We _____ an exercise plan together.

Carla: How did that work?

Jun: We _____ cooperatively. We _____ on Skype

and _____ our ideas on Google Docs. Then we made a slide

show.

Carla: That does sound kind of fun.

Jun: Yeah. And we _____ our slide shows to students in the PE

department. Everyone _____ a lot of questions. My English really

_____. In fact, I'm taking another English class this summer.

Carla: You're kidding!

Jun: No. Mr. Conner's teaching another class. I _____ to take as many

of his classes as I can!

GO ONLINE
to practice the
conversation

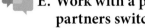 **D. Practice the conversation in Activity C with a partner.**

E. Work with a partner. Partner A asks a question. Partner B answers correctly. Then partners switch roles.

1. a. We post our stories online.   What social media site do you use?
   b. We posted our stories online.   Did people write comments on them?

2. a. I play for the Giants.   Are you on a team this year, too?
   b. I played for the Giants.   That's a good way to keep fit!

3. a. They want to come with us.   Yes, but they had a better time at home.
   b. They wanted to come with us.   Sure. There's plenty of room in the car.

4. a. We need to get some fresh air and exercise.   I know, but we need to study for the test more!
   b. We needed to get some fresh air and exercise.   Yeah, let's go on a bike ride today!

A. Think about times when you worked with other people on a team. What was the situation? What did you do together? Were you successful? What did you learn? Write notes in the chart.

My team experience (Was it a sports team, a particular game, a school or work project?)	What was the goal?	What happened? (How well did you work together? Did you achieve your goal? Why or why not?)	What did you learn?

Word Partners

be on a team

be a member of a team

be part of a team

join a team

play on a team

GO ONLINE
to practice
word partners

Speaking Skill

Using past time markers in stories

Speakers use past time markers in stories to show the time they are talking about. Listen to the examples.

> *Last summer*, I worked in a big office downtown.
>
> *In 2002*, I decided to leave home and study in Canada.
>
> *A long time ago*, I played volleyball on a school team.
>
> *When I was in high school*, I had a teacher I really liked.
>
> *Before I came here*, I didn't speak any English.

 B. Work with a partner. Tell your partner about your team experiences. Decide which one is the most interesting and which one is the easiest to explain.

 C. Make a list of things you did in the past. Use the verbs in the box or your own ideas. Then tell your partner about your past. Use the past tense markers in the Speaking Skill box.

learned	played	saw	studied	traveled	visited	went

Speaking Task

Describing a team experience

1. Look at your notes in Step 2. Organize your ideas in the chart.

What was the experience?	
What was the goal?	
What happened?	
What did you learn?	

2. Close your book. Work in a group. Tell your group about your team experience. Give as much information as you can. Listen to your group members' team experiences and ask questions.

Step 3 REPORT

A. Think about your group members' experiences. Write notes in the chart.

1. Who had the most successful team experience? Why was it successful?	
2. Who learned the most useful lesson?	
3. What story was the most interesting? Why was it the most interesting?	

B. Share your notes. Which story was the most interesting?

Step 4 REFLECT

Checklist

Check (✓) the things you learned in Chapter 5.

○ I learned language for talking about teams.

○ I understood someone telling a story.

○ I described a team experience.

Discussion Question

What are your personal tips on how to work in a team?

CHAPTER 6 What Was It Like?

- Use *was* and *were*
- Listen for ways speakers show interest and understanding
- Recognize contractions of *wasn't* and *weren't*
- Listen for problems and solutions
- Practice linking *was/wasn't/were/weren't* with vowels
- Describe how a change made life better, safer, or healthier

▲ VOCABULARY ► Oxford 2000 🗝 words to talk about healthy environments

Learn Words

🔊 **A. Label each picture with the correct words. Then listen and repeat the phrases.**

| beautiful | ~~clean~~ | convenient | fresh | healthy | large | local | safe |

1.

_____clean_____ air and a

_____ environment

2.

_____ public transportation

to a _____ shopping mall

3.

_____ streets and a

_____ public park

4.

_____ fruits and vegetables

at a _____ farmers' market

Grammar Note

was and were

🔊 Speakers use the simple past form of *be* to describe people, things, locations, and conditions in the past. Listen to the examples.

*What **was** the air like in the 1960s?* →	*In the 1960s, the air **was** bad. It **wasn't** clean.*
*How **were** the public parks in the past?* →	*The public parks **were** smaller. They **weren't** fun.*
***Was** the downtown area nice?* →	*No, the downtown area **wasn't** nice. It **was** crowded.*
***Were** the shops busy a long time ago?* →	*Yes, they **were**. People bought everything at small shops.*

🔊 **B. Listen and check (✓) the phrase you hear.**

1. ☐	*The game is*	✓	*The game was*	on Saturday afternoon.
2. ☐	*The fruit at the store is*	☐	*The fruit at the store was*	fresh.
3. ☐	*The farmers' market isn't*	☐	*The farmers' market wasn't*	large.
4. ☐	*The parks aren't*	☐	*The parks weren't*	open at night.
5. ☐	*The streets are*	☐	*The streets were*	safe for children.
6. ☐	*The shopping mall isn't*	☐	*The shopping mall wasn't*	very convenient.

🔊 **C. Listen and repeat each question and answer.**

1. Where was your school?	It was far away. I took a bus to get there.
2. Were you on a team?	Yes, I was. I was on the soccer team.
3. Was your town small?	No, it wasn't. It was large.
4. Was the air clean?	Yes, it was. I lived near the beach.
5. How were the public parks?	They were nice. There were a lot of things to do at the parks.
6. What was the food like?	It was great! There was a lot of fresh food.

 D. Work with a partner. Think about your childhood. Partner A asks a question from Activity C. Partner B answers. Then partners switch roles.

Learn Phrases

A. Match each phrase to the correct picture. Then listen and repeat.

downtown is **a car-free area**	**make improvements** to public parks
add green space to the city	make the roads **less crowded**
create a healthy environment for children	**make the streets safe** for pedestrians
have better **air quality**	**put in** bike paths

1.

2.

3.

4.

5.

6.

7.

8.

B. Listen to the conversations. Match the phrases with the situations.

a. make the roads less crowded and make the streets safe for pedestrians

b. add green space to the city

c. ~~have better air quality~~

d. downtown is a car-free area with bike paths

e. create a healthy environment for children

f. make improvements to a public park

Situation 1: ___c___

Situation 2: _____

Situation 3: _____

Situation 4: _____

Situation 5: _____

Situation 6: _____

C. Work with a partner. Talk about your neighborhood, town, or city. Ask and answer the questions. Explain your answers.

1. Are the streets safe for pedestrians?

2. Does your neighborhood have a healthy environment for children?

3. Does your city have good air quality?

4. Does your city have bike paths?

5. Do you have a car-free area?

6. Are the roads crowded?

Are the streets safe for pedestrians?

Yes, they are.

Why are they safe?

There are a lot of places to cross the roads.

GO ONLINE
for more
practice

▲▲ LISTENING

CONVERSATION

🔊 **A. Listen to the conversation. Who are the speakers? Check (✓) the correct answer.**

☐ two people about the same age from the same family

☐ a young person and an old person from the same family

☐ a young person and an old person from different families

🔊 **B. Listen to the conversation again. Does the information describe Cedar City now or in the past? Circle *Now* or *Past*.**

1. no public parks	*Now*	*Past*
2. a farmers' market	*Now*	*Past*
3. place to get fresh food	*Now*	*Past*
4. traffic	*Now*	*Past*

Listening Strategy

Listening for ways speakers show interest and understanding

🔊 Speakers often ask questions in a conversation. They ask for more information about a topic, and they ask questions to make sure they understand information. These questions show that they are interested. Listen to the examples.

A: *There were a lot of small shops.*   A: *There was a lot more traffic then.*

B: **There wasn't a shopping mall?**   B: **What do you mean?**

A: *No, there wasn't.*   A: *There were more cars on the road.*

GO ONLINE
for more
practice

🔊 **C. Listen to the conversation again. What ideas does Alan ask questions about? Check (✓) the correct answers.**

☐ Cedar City is a much nicer place now.

☐ The houses were too expensive.

☐ Life in Cedar City is a lot healthier now.

☐ The air was bad, too.

Contractions of *wasn't* and *weren't*

🔊 Speakers usually use contractions with *was + not* and *were + not*. Listen to the examples.

*The weather **was not** warm.* → *The weather **wasn't** warm.*

*The buses **were not** comfortable.* → *The buses **weren't** comfortable.*

Was the train late? → *No, it **wasn't**. It was on time.*

Were the vegetables fresh? → *No, they **weren't**. They **weren't** very nice.*

🔊 **D. Listen and check (✓) the statement you hear.**

1. ☐ The market wasn't open.   ✓ The markets weren't open.

2. ☐ The street wasn't clean.   ☐ The streets weren't clean.

3. ☐ The bus wasn't convenient.   ☐ The buses weren't convenient.

4. ☐ The phone wasn't new.   ☐ The phones weren't new.

5. ☐ The team wasn't successful.   ☐ The teams weren't successful.

6. ☐ The park wasn't beautiful.   ☐ The parks weren't beautiful.

🔊 **E. Complete each conversation with the contracted form of *was + not* or *were + not*. Then listen and check your answers.**

1. A: Was Marta at the meeting?

   B: No, she _____. She was at the gym.

2. A: The parks _____ safe a few years ago.

   B: I know. We didn't have a good place for kids to play then.

3. A: Was the city quiet when you were young?

   B: No, it _____. It was very noisy.

4. A: How was your bike ride?

   B: It _____ very nice. The air was bad.

5. A: How were the farmers' markets in New York?

   B: They _____ bad. In fact, they were pretty good!

6. A: There _____ bike paths in this city when I was a child.

   B: I know. Bike riding was dangerous then!

Chant

GO ONLINE for the Chapter 6 Vocabulary and Grammar Chant

A. What are some things that make towns and cities healthy places to live? Check (✓) the things and add your own ideas.

☐ public parks   ☐ safe streets

☐ clean air   ☐ _____

☐ farmers' markets   ☐ _____

B. Work as a group to discuss your ideas in Activity A. Share your ideas with the class. Then discuss your answers to the question.

Which of the things in Activity A do you have in your town or city?

C. Listen to the introduction. What are the speakers talking about? Circle the correct answer.

results of a plan to   *a plan for the future*   *problems a city had in*
improve a city   *of a city*   *the past*

Listening Strategy

Listening for problems and solutions

🔊 Speakers use certain words and expressions to introduce problems and solutions, answers to problems or ways to fix them. Listen to the examples.

> **There was a problem with** bicycle accidents. More bike paths **solved this problem.**
>
> **One issue was** bad public transportation. **We fixed this issue** with more bus lines.

D. Listen to the rest of the presentation. Circle the solutions for each problem. There is more than one correct solution for each problem.

1. There were accidents in the downtown area. The solution was to

plant trees.   *make the downtown area car-free.*   *add bike paths.*

2. The air was bad. The solution was to

make the park bigger.   *add bike paths.*   *plant trees.*

3. People weren't fit. The solution was to

plant trees.   *make the downtown area car-free.*   *add bike paths.*

GO ONLINE
for more
practice

E. Listen to the main part of the presentation again. Circle the correct answers.

1. Cars *can* *can't* go into a car-free area.

2. There *are* *aren't* a lot of cars on the road in Cedar City now.

3. The city *made the park bigger* *built a new park.*

4. The city planted more than *200* *100* trees.

F. Listen to the presentation again. Then ask and answer the questions with a partner.

Partner A	Partner B
1. What was the downtown area like in the past?	2. What is the downtown area like now?
3. What makes the downtown area safe for bicyclists?	4. What is one thing that made the air cleaner?
5. What is another thing that made the air cleaner?	6. Why are people in Cedar City healthier now?

Discuss the Ideas

H. Work with a partner. Use the phrases in the chart and your own ideas to discuss cities.

Partner A	Partner B	Partner A	Partner B	
What's your favorite city?	My favorite city is…	Why is it your favorite?	It's…	beautiful.
			The city is…	clean.
			The food is…	convenient.
			The parks are…	fresh.
			The people are…	friendly.
			The downtown area is…	good.
				great.
			The air is…	healthy.
				large.
				local.
				safe.

What's your favorite city?

My favorite city is Portland.

Why is it your favorite?

It's safe, and the food is great.

▲▲▲ SPEAKING

Speaking Task Describing how a change made life better, safer, or healthier

Step 1 PREPARE

Pronunciation Skill

Linking *was/wasn't/were/weren't* with vowels

◀)) Speakers link the final consonant sound in *was*, *wasn't*, *were*, and *weren't* with the first vowel sound in the word that follows. Listen to the examples.

Lucie **was a** student in 2016.	→	Lucie wa**za** student in 2016.
There **wasn't a** gym here when I was a child.	→	There wasn'**ta** gym here when I was a child.
There **were accidents** in the downtown area.	→	There we**raccidents** in the downtown area.
There **weren't a** lot of cars here a long time ago.	→	There weren'**ta** lot of cars here a long time ago.

GO ONLINE for more practice

◀)) **A. Listen and repeat.**

1. apps	were apps	They were apps for fitness.
2. a market	was a market	There was a market every Sunday.
3. a bike path	wasn't a bike path	There wasn't a bike path here last year.
4. a lot of accidents	weren't a lot of accidents	There weren't a lot of accidents.
5. an engineer	was an engineer	Shanika was an engineer.
6. a break	wasn't a break	There wasn't a break after lunch.

◀)) **B. Listen. Check (✓) the sentence you hear.**

1. [✓] There were a lot of people at the gym today.　　[ ] There weren't a lot of people at the gym today.

2. [ ] That wasn't a very good idea.　　[ ] That was a very good idea.

3. [ ] There was a plan to improve the downtown area.　　[ ] There wasn't a plan to improve the downtown area.

4. [ ] Public transportation was a problem.　　[ ] Public transportation wasn't a problem.

C. Listen. Complete the conversation with the words from the box. Responses may be used more than once.

was	wasn't	were	weren't

Kenji: So, what _____ the school like when you were here?

Amy: It _____ a great place to study, but it _____ attractive.

Kenji: What do you mean?

Amy: Well, there _____ tall buildings, and there _____ a big parking lot. That's about all. It _____ ugly actually!

Kenji: Wow. The campus is so nice now. There are lots of trees and plants and nice places to walk.

Amy: Well, back then, there _____ any trees. There _____ enough grass, either.

Kenji: What else?

Amy: It _____ actually very safe then, either.

Kenji: What do you mean?

Amy: There _____ a lot of bike accidents. People rode their bikes everywhere—in the streets, on the sidewalks. It was dangerous. So the college put in bike paths. Now it's safer for bicyclists and pedestrians.

Kenji: What else?

Amy: Umm, let me see… Oh, there _____ a place to run or play basketball. It's a much safer and healthier environment now.

GO ONLINE
to practice the
conversation

D. Work with a partner. Practice the conversation in Activity C.

E. Work with a partner. Partner A asks a question. Partner B answers correctly. Then partners switch roles.

1. a. My neighborhood was attractive and safe.   Oh, that's too bad.
   b. My neighborhood wasn't attractive.   Oh, how nice!

2. a. There weren't a lot of trees then.   I know, but we have a very nice one now.
   b. There wasn't a farmers' market then.   I know. The air quality wasn't very good.

3. a. They were excited about the new park.   Yes. Now the kids have a nice place to play.
   b. They weren't excited about the new buildings.   I know. That area isn't very attractive now.

A. Think about some places you know well (in your country, city, school, or other places). What were they like in the past? What are they like now? Are they better or worse? How? Use the chart to take notes.

Place	What was it like in the past?	What is it like now?	Is it better or worse now?

 B. Work with a group. Tell the group about your places. Which place is better because of the changes? How is it better?

Speaking Skill

Describing problems and solutions

🔊 Speakers use words and expressions to describe problems and their solutions. Listen to the examples.

There was a problem with *the gym. It was too small. The school* ***solved the problem****. It made the gym bigger.*

One issue was *the traffic downtown. The city* ***fixed the problem****. Now the downtown area is car-free.*

 C. Look at the problems and solutions in the chart. Add more problems and solutions. Then describe the problems and solutions to a partner. Use the expressions in the Speaking Skill box.

Problems	Solutions
traffic	improve public transportation
bad air	build parks
_____	_____
_____	_____

Speaking Task Describing how a change made life better, safer, or healthier

1. With your group, choose a place from your notes in Step 2. Explain how the place is better, safer, or healthier now because of improvements. Organize your ideas in the chart.

What is the place?	
What was it like before? What were the problems?	
What is it like now? What were the solutions?	
How is it better, safer, or healthier now?	

2. With your group members, practice explaining how your place improved.

3. Work with another group. Close your books. Tell the other group about your place. Give as much information as you can. Listen to the other group's explanation and ask questions.

Step 3 REPORT

A. Choose one group's explanation. Write notes about the place in the chart.

Place	Problems	Solutions

B. Discuss your notes in Activity A as a class. Which placed changed the most?

Step 4 REFLECT

Checklist

Check (✓) the things you learned in Chapter 6.

○ I learned language for talking about healthy environments.

○ I understood speakers describing problems and solutions.

○ I described how a place got better.

Discussion Question

Where is the best place to live? What makes it the best place for you?

Look at the word bank for Unit 2. Check (✓) the words you know. Circle the words you want to learn better.

OXFORD 2000 🔑

Adjectives	Nouns		Verbs	
beautiful	air	key	achieve	make
clean	attitude	schedule	add	play
convenient	energy	shape	burn	practice
different	environment	space	create	put
fast	heart	street	do	ride
fresh	image	success	fit	see
green	improvement	thing	get	take on
healthy	job	way	give	watch
large			go	win
local			have	work
positive			learn	
safe				

PRACTICE WITH THE OXFORD 2000 🔑

A. Use the chart. Match adjectives with nouns.

1. _____ fresh air _____   2. _____

3. _____   4. _____

5. _____   6. _____

B. Use the chart. Match verbs with nouns.

1. _____ achieve success _____   2. _____

3. _____   4. _____

5. _____   6. _____

C. Use the chart. Match verbs with adjective noun partners.

1. _____ have safe streets _____   2. _____

3. _____   4. _____

5. _____   6. _____

UNIT 3 Travel and Tourism

CHAPTER 7 Where Were You Going?

▲ **VOCABULARY**
- Oxford 2000 🔑 words to talk about travel

▲▲▲ **LISTENING**
- Listening for tone and attitude
- Listening to take notes with a mind map

▲▲▲▲ **SPEAKING**
- Linking *wh-* questions words with *was/were*
- Describing an unusual or surprising travel experience

CHAPTER 8 Why Should You Go There?

▲ **VOCABULARY**
- Oxford 2000 🔑 words to talk about important places

▲▲▲ **LISTENING**
- Listening for specific details
- Listening for causes and effects

▲▲▲▲ **SPEAKING**
- Reducing *have to* and *has to*
- Describing an important place and explaining why we should protect it

CHAPTER 9 Are You Interested in Adventure?

▲ **VOCABULARY**
- Oxford 2000 🔑 words to talk about adventure

▲▲▲ **LISTENING**
- Recognizing promotional language
- Listening to take notes with a T-chart

▲▲▲▲ **SPEAKING**
- Practicing sentence stress
- Presenting a position in a debate

UNIT WRAP UP Extend Your Skills

- Use the past progressive
- Listen for tone and attitude
- Recognize the reduction of *-ing* with the past progressive
- Listen to take notes with a mind map
- Link *wh-* question words with *was/were*
- Describe an unusual or surprising travel experience

▲ **VOCABULARY** ► Oxford 2000 🔑 words to talk about travel

Learn Words

🔊 **A. Label each picture with the correct words. Then listen and repeat the phrases.**

| exploring | having | learning about | looking for | shopping | speaking | staying | visiting |

1.

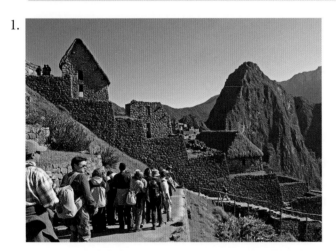

_____visiting_____ an ancient site and

_____ the culture

2.

_____ for souvenirs and

_____ bargains

3.

_____ the town and

_____ the language

4.

_____ in a hotel and

_____ a great time

Grammar Note

The past progressive

Speakers use the past progressive to describe actions that were in progress in the past. Listen to the examples.

I'm studying Korean. → *Last year, I* **was studying** *Japanese.*

She's traveling in Canada. → *She* **was traveling** *in Australia last spring.*

They're playing volleyball. → *They* **were playing** *basketball earlier.*

To ask questions, speakers use *was/were* before the subject. Listen to the examples.

A: **Were** *you* **teaching** *art last year?*   *B: No, I* **wasn't.** *I* **was teaching** *music.*

A: What **was** *she* **buying**?   *B: She* **was buying** *souvenirs.*

B. Listen and repeat.

1. Was Samir visiting an ancient site? Yes, he was. He was taking pictures of a very old church.

2. What were you doing last year? I was traveling in Canada.

3. Was Rachel learning Japanese? No, she wasn't. She was studying Korean.

4. Were you exploring the city? Yes, I was, but I got lost!

5. Where were they playing soccer? They were playing soccer at Cedar College.

6. Was Ali having a good time? Yes, he was. He was having a great time on his vacation.

7. How was Ron feeling? He was happy. He wasn't feeling lonely or sad.

8. Were they shopping for souvenirs? Yes, they were. They bought some T-shirts at a market.

C. Work with a partner. Ask and answer the questions in Activity B.

D. Listen and check (✓) the statement you hear.

1. [✓] He's learning about the culture.   [ ] He was learning about the culture.

2. [ ] We're speaking Spanish.   [ ] We were speaking Spanish.

3. [ ] They're playing basketball.   [ ] They were playing basketball.

4. [ ] She's staying at a nice hotel.   [ ] She was staying at a nice hotel.

5. [ ] I'm having a great time.   [ ] I was having a great time.

6. [ ] He's looking for bargains.   [ ] He was looking for bargains.

Learn Phrases

A. Match each phrase to the correct picture. Then listen and repeat.

ask directions in **the local language**	**taking pictures** of a fountain
learn how to **make local dishes**	travel that **helps the local economy**
see **different types of animals and plants**	travel that is **good for the environment**
stay **in a forest**	walking around **the old part of town**

1.

2.

3.

4.

5.

6.

7.

8.

B. Listen to each conversation. Circle the correct answer.

1. The speaker is describing	*the old part of town.*	*different types of animals and plants.*
2. The speaker is	*asking directions in the local language.*	*learning how to make local dishes.*
3. The speaker is describing	*travel that is good for the environment.*	*travel that helps the local economy.*
4. The speaker is talking about	*travel that helps the local economy.*	*travel that is good for the environment.*
5. The speaker is talking about	*different types of animals and plants.*	*how to make a local dish.*
6. The speakers are in	*a forest.*	*the old part of town.*

C. Read each situation. Circle your answer. Then ask and answer the questions with a partner.

1. You are in a different country and you are lost. What do you do?

ask directions in my language   *ask directions in the local language*   *don't ask for directions*

2. You are walking around a new city. What do you want to do?

see old buildings   *visit museums*   *take pictures of statues and fountains*

3. A friend wants to have a vacation in a forest and see different types of animals and plants. You…

like vacations in natural places   *only like vacations in big cities*   *like to stay in a comfortable hotel*

4. You want a vacation that is…

good for the environment   *educational*   *fun*

5. On a vacation, you like to…

learn new things   *try the local food*   *see important sites*

D. Circle two words or phrases that pair with each verb.

1. ask	*for directions*	*for help*	*a local dish*
2. learn	*pictures*	*a language*	*to cook*
3. see	*sights*	*animals*	*the economy*
4. stay	*home*	*pictures*	*in a forest*
5. take	*sights*	*a trip*	*pictures*
6. walk	*around*	*the economy*	*to the beach*

GO ONLINE
for more
practice

▲▲ LISTENING

CONVERSATION

🔊 **A. Listen to the conversation. What is the story about? Circle the correct answer.**

a shopping experience   *a school experience*   *a travel experience*

🔊 **B. Listen to the conversation again. Circle the correct answer to complete each statement.**

1. Sam was taking pictures of   *some people.   a fountain.*

2. He met some people, and they stayed together for   *a few   five*   days.

3. Sam and his friends were shopping for   *food   souvenirs*   in the market.

4. Sam's   *wallet   key*   was missing.

GO ONLINE
for more
practice

Listening Strategy

Listening for tone and attitude

🔊 Speakers use certain words and phrases to express emotions. Speakers use these words to express feelings such as surprise, sadness, happiness, and sympathy. (*Sympathy* is sharing another person's feelings.) Listen to the examples.

Expression	Meaning
Oh! Gosh! Wow!	I'm surprised!
Uh-oh. Oh, no! Oh, dear!	That's sounds bad. I feel sad for you.
Nice! Cool! Great!	That's sounds good. I'm happy for you!

🔊 **C. Listen to each conversation. Circle the expression you hear.**

1. A: We were playing soccer with the Tigers last Saturday, and we won!
   B: *Cool!   Great!*

2. A: I was exploring the city, and I fell down!
   B: *Oh, dear!   Oh, no!*

3. A: We were hungry, and we found a really great restaurant.
   B: *Cool!   Nice!*

 D. Work with a partner. In each conversation in Activity C, discuss how Speaker B is feeling. Use the meanings in the Listening Strategy box.

Reduction of *-ing* with the past progressive

 When speakers use the past progressive, the *-ing* verb ending sometimes sounds like *n*. Listen to the examples.

> We were **visiting** a museum. → We were **visitin** a museum.
>
> Where were you **going**? → Where were you **goin**?

E. Listen and check (✓) the sentence you hear.

1. ☐ They were studying art last year.
   ☑ They were studyin art last year.

2. ☐ We were using public transportation to get to school.
   ☐ We were usin public transportation to get to school.

3. ☐ Sam was taking pictures of an old building.
   ☐ Sam was takin pictures of an old building.

4. ☐ Ali was watching a basketball game on TV last Saturday.
   ☐ Ali was watchin a basketball game on TV last Saturday.

5. ☐ The city was putting in bike paths last summer.
   ☐ The city was puttin in bike paths last summer.

F. Work with a partner. Partner A says a sentence from Activity E. Partner B points to the correct sentence. Then partners switch roles.

G. Listen and circle the words you hear.

1. What were you   *studying* (*doing*) last summer?
2. What were you   *watching*   *studying*   last year?
3. How were you   *getting*   *going*   to school last week?
4. Where were you   *living*   *studying*   five years ago?
5. Who were you   *listening*   *talking*   to last night?

H. Work with a partner. Ask and answer the questions in Activity G.

Chant

GO ONLINE for the Chapter 7 Vocabulary and Grammar Chant

ACADEMIC LISTENING

A. Work with a partner. What are some reasons that people travel? Check (✓) the reasons and add your own idea.

☐ to learn something about history or culture

☐ to play sports (like golf or surfing)

☐ to practice a new language

☐ to visit friends or family

☐ to relax

☐ _____

B. Work as a group to discuss your ideas in Activity A. Share your ideas with the class. Then discuss your answers to the question.

Why do you travel?

C. Listen to the first part of the presentation. What is the topic? Circle the correct answer.

The presentation is about travel that...

is safe for travelers.   *helps the place you visit.*   *is fun and relaxing.*

Listening Strategy

Listening to take notes with a mind map

It's important to take notes when you are listening to an academic presentation. One way to take notes is with a mind map. Mind maps help you organize main ideas and details. Listen to the speaker and study the mind map.

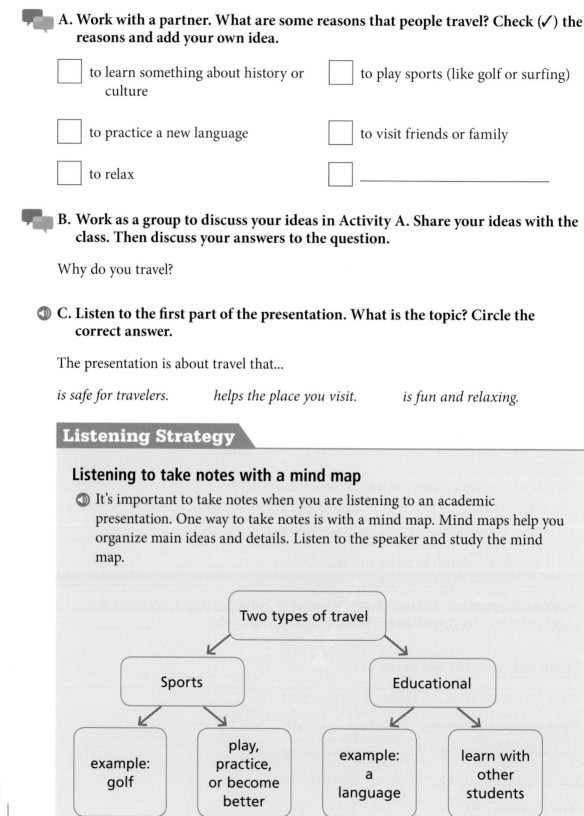

GO ONLINE
for more
practice

D. Listen to the second part of the presentation. Complete the left side of the mind map with details from the box.

cut down trees   Hawaii   kill fish   make money

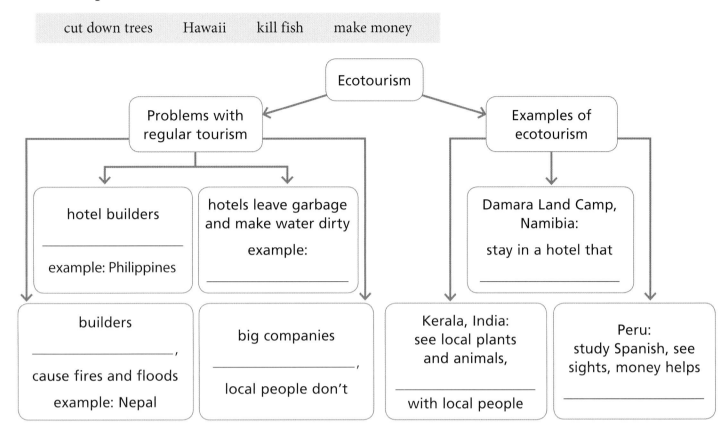

E. Listen to the third part of the presentation. Complete the right side of the mind map in Activity D with details from the box.

fish and cook   local people built   a school

F. Listen to the entire presentation. Then ask and answer the questions with a partner.

Partner A	Partner B
1. What is ecotourism?	2. Why do we need ecotourism?
3. What are some examples of tourism that is bad for the environment?	4. How is regular tourism bad for local people?
5. What is one example of ecotourism?	6. What is another example of ecotourism?

Discuss the Ideas

G. Work with a group. What are some ways that you can make any trip an "ecotrip"? Discuss your ideas.

Speaking Task

Describing an unusual or surprising travel experience

Step 1 PREPARE

Pronunciation Skill

Linking *wh-* question words with *was/were*

🔊 When speakers ask *wh-* questions in the past progressive, they often link the final consonant sound in the *wh-* word with the consonant sound at the beginning of *was* and *were*. Listen to the examples.

What were you doing? → *Wha**tw**ere you doing?*

Where was he going? → *Whe**rew**as he going?*

Who were you visiting? → *Wh**ow**ere you visiting?*

When was she leaving? → *Whe**nw**as she leaving?*

GO ONLINE
for more
practice

🔊 **A. Listen and repeat.**

1. What	What were	What were they studying?
2. When	When was	When was he visiting Japan?
3. Where	Where were	Where were they playing?
4. Who	Who was	Who was she calling?
5. How	How were	How were they getting there?
6. Where	Where was	Where was he driving?
7. What	What were	What were you looking for?
8. Who	Who were	Who were they working with?

 B. Work with a partner. Partner A says a question from Activity A. Partner B points to the correct question. Then partners switch roles.

🔊 **C. Listen to each conversation. Check (✓) the phrase the speaker links.**

1. ☐ what were   ✓ where were

2. ☐ where was   ☐ who was

3. ☐ how were   ☐ when were

4. ☐ what was   ☐ who was

D. Listen. Use the phrases from the box to complete the conversations.

| How was | What was | When were | Where was | Who were | Why were |

1. A: Did you know that Paolo was in Korea last week?
   B: No. _____What was_____ he doing there?
   A: He was traveling there for business.

2. A: Lara had a great time in Hawaii.
   B: Oh, I love Hawaii. _____ she staying?
   A: At a hotel on Maui.

3. A: They told us that the market was this way.
   B: But now we're lost! _____ you talking to?
   A: A police officer, but I don't understand Spanish very well!

4. A: _____ you visiting your aunt?
   B: She broke her arm, and I wanted to help her around the house.

5. A: I saw Luis last week.
   B: _____ he feeling?
   A: Much better! He feels great, in fact.

6. A: I taught English in Costa Rica for a while. I loved it there!
   B: Nice! _____ you working there?
   A: In 2015.

GO ONLINE
to practice the
conversations

E. Work with a partner. Practice the conversations in Activity D.

F. Work with a partner. Partner A asks a question. Partner B answers correctly. Then partners switch roles.

1. a. Where was he going?   To a museum.
   b. What was he doing?   He was asking directions.

2. a. What were you studying?   Because we have a test tomorrow.
   b. Why were you studying?   Computer science.

3. a. Who were you talking to?   Marta Gomez.
   b. Where were you talking?   In the gym.

4. a. What were you looking for?   At the farmers' market.
   b. Where were you shopping?   Some bargains.

5. a. When were you visiting your dad? I really miss him!
   b. Why were you visiting your dad?   Last summer.

6. a. What were you doing in the old part of town?   Souvenirs.
   b. What were you buying in the old part of town?   I was taking pictures.

A. Think about one or more travel experiences. Where did you go? What happened? Use the chart to take notes. Then discuss your chart with a partner.

Where did you go?	When did you go?	What did you see? What did you do?	Did anything unusual or surprising happen?

Speaking Skill

Making a story more exciting

Speakers use words and expressions to make events in a story sound exciting. Expressions such as *all of a sudden, suddenly,* and *unexpectedly* show surprise. Listen to the example.

I was walking down the street, and I saw a small shop. The shop had wonderful souvenirs. I decided to buy some. I reached into my backpack to get my wallet. **Suddenly**, *I felt something move in my backpack. I looked in, and I saw a mouse!*

B. Listen and complete each conversation with the words you hear.

1. A: I was walking down the street in a small town in Mexico. _____, I saw my best friend from grade school!

   B: That's amazing!

2. A: Then what happened?

   B: We were sitting down at a table in a nice restaurant. _____, I noticed that my credit card was missing.

3. A: We were playing volleyball on the beach. We were having a lot of fun. _____, I slipped and fell.

   B: Oh, dear!

4. A: I was walking around the old part of town. I was taking pictures. _____, I realized that I was lost!

   B: Oh, no!

Word Partners

a business trip

an overseas trip

a short trip

a nice trip

a sightseeing trip

a school trip

GO ONLINE
to practice
word partners

Speaking Task Describing an unusual or surprising travel experience

1. Choose a travel experience from your notes in Step 2. Tell where you went, when you went there, and what you did. Also, describe anything unusual or surprising that happened. Organize your ideas in the chart.

Where did you go?	
When did you go?	
What did you see? What did you do?	
Did anything unusual or surprising happen?	

2. Practice describing your travel experience with two or three partners.

3. Work in a group. Close your books. Tell your group about your travel experience. Give as much information as you can. Listen to your partners' travel experiences and ask questions.

Step 3 REPORT

A. Think about your partners' stories. Write notes in the chart.

1. Who had the most unusual or surprising travel experience?	
2. Why was it unusual or surprising?	

B. Share your notes. Which story was the most interesting? Why?

Step 4 REFLECT

Checklist

Check (✓) the things you learned in Chapter 7.

○ I learned language for talking about travel.

○ I understood someone telling a story.

○ I described an unusual or surprising travel experience.

Discussion Question

What are some things that you can learn from a travel experience?

CHAPTER 8

Why Should You Go There?

- Use modals of necessity and advice
- Listen for specific details
- Recognize the reduction of *have to*, *need to*, and *ought to*

- Listen for causes and effects
- Practice reducing *have to* and *has to*
- Describe an important place and explain why we should protect it

▲ VOCABULARY ▶ Oxford 2000 ⚷ words to talk about important places

Learn Words

🔊 **A. Label each picture with the correct word. Then listen and repeat the words and phrases.**

| art | ~~building~~ | church | city | forest | garden | structures | wonder |

1.

an important _____building_____

2.

a famous _____

3.

huge _____

4.

an ancient _____

5.

a natural _____

6.

a historic _____

7.

a damaged _____

8.

a valuable work of _____

Grammar Note

Modals of necessity and advice

Speakers use certain modals + a verb to express necessity and advice. Listen to the examples.

Necessity

You **have to** get to class on time.

We **need to** leave at noon. We don't want to miss the bus.

Advice

You **should** take a nap. You look tired.

We **ought to** save some money. Travel is expensive.

To ask questions with *have to, need to,* and *ought to,* speakers use *do/does* before the subject. (Note: Speakers rarely ask questions with *ought to.*) To ask questions with *should,* speakers use *should* before the subject. Listen to the examples.

A: Do you **have to** leave now?

B: Yes, I do. I'm going to be late.

A: Why does he **need to** study computer science?

B: So he can get a good job.

A: **Should** I visit Japan in the fall?

B: Yes, you should. The weather is nice in the fall.

A: Where **should** I go on my vacation?

B: You ought to go to Hawaii. It's very relaxing.

B. Listen and repeat.

1. You should save money.

2. People have to be careful in crowded areas.

3. We ought to visit the forest.

4. Raul should take pictures for his blog.

5. I have to learn some Spanish.

6. You ought to see the huge structures.

7. Lara needs to see to the garden.

8. We need to go there soon.

C. Listen and repeat each question and answer.

Questions	Answers
1. Why should we visit Rome?	Because it's a beautiful city.
2. Do we need to bring our camera?	No. My phone takes great pictures.
3. Do we have to take public transportation?	Yes. It's good for the environment.
4. When do you need to go?	I don't have to go yet. It's still early.
5. Does Jun have to bring a jacket?	No, but he ought to bring a sweater. It's cool at night.

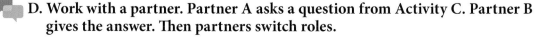

D. Work with a partner. Partner A asks a question from Activity C. Partner B gives the answer. Then partners switch roles.

Learn Phrases

🔊 **A. Match each phrase to the correct picture. Then listen and repeat.**

a famous landmark **in my city**	ancient structures **tell us about the past**
a natural disaster such as climate change	**protect** a national treasure
a natural wonder **at risk**	**tear down** a historic building

1.

_____

2.

_____

3.

_____

4.

_____

5.

_____

6.

_____

B. Listen to each conversation. What is the speaker talking about? Circle the letter of the correct answer.

1. a. a structure that tells us about the past
   b. a natural wonder at risk

2. a. a famous landmark
   b. climate change

3. a. an ancient site that told her about the past
   b. tearing down a historic building

4. a. an ancient structure
   b. climate change

5. a. tearing down a historic building
   b. climate change

6. a. protecting a national treasure
   b. a natural wonder at risk

C. Complete the sentences about your town or city. Then tell your partner about your town or city. Ask your partner about his or her town or city.

1. In my   town   city,   people want to   tear down   protect   an old building.

2. We have a famous landmark in my   town   city.   It's called _____.

3. We   have   do not have   an ancient structure in my   town   city.

4. Climate change   is   is not   a problem in my   town.   city.

5. We have a natural wonder in my   town   city.   It's   a   an   _____.

> In my city, people want to protect an old building.

> Really? What is it?

> It's an old bank. It's a really beautiful building.

D. Work with a partner. Partner A describes a famous landmark. Partner B guesses the landmark. Then partners switch roles.

> It's big and orange. You can drive or walk over it. You can see the Pacific Ocean from it.

> Is it the Golden Gate Bridge?

> That's right!

GO ONLINE
for more
practice

▲▲ LISTENING

CONVERSATION

🔊 **A. Listen to the conversation. Where are the speakers talking about something interesting to see? Circle the correct answer.**

on an island   *in a museum*   *in a city*

🔊 **B. Listen to the conversation again. Circle the correct answer to complete each statement.**

1. Mike is talking about a vacation that he   *will have in the future.*   *had in the past.*

2. The place has   *famous structures.*   *a huge forest.*

3. Layla should go there because the place is going to be   *crowded*   *expensive*   soon.

Listening Strategy

Listening for specific details

🔊 Speakers often ask for and give each other specific details when they are discussing an interesting topic. Details describe how something looks, sounds, tastes, smells, or feels. Listen to the examples.

Asking for details	**Giving details**
What does it look like?	*It looks like a huge head.*
What is it like?	*It is soft and round.*
What are they like?	*They're green and smell really nice.*

GO ONLINE for more practice

 C. Work with a partner. Practice asking for details. Partner A tells Partner B about an interesting building or landmark. Partner B asks for details. Then partners switch roles.

🔊 **D. Listen to part of the conversation again. Check (✓) details about the *moai*, the structures that Mike describes.**

1. How many heads are there?
a. 900
b. 500

2. How tall are the heads?
a. 23 feet
b. 32 feet

3. Where are the heads?
a. They are all over the place.
b. They are all in one place.

4. How much does each head weigh?
a. 14 tons
b. 40 tons

5. What do the heads look like?

a. They all have the same expression on their faces, and they are all fat.

b. They have different expressions on their faces. Some are fat, and some are thin.

Reduction of *have to*, *need to*, and *ought to*

When speakers use *have to*, *need to*, and *ought to*, the *to* sometimes sounds like *ta*. Listen to the examples.

The *v* in *have to* sounds like *f* when you reduce it.

You **have to** go now. → You **hafta** go now.

He **has to** come with us. → He **hasta** come with us.

She **needs to** see this. → She **needsta** see this.

We **need to** see it soon. → We **needta** see it soon.

She **ought to** come home. → She **oughta** come home.

E. Listen and check (✓) the sentence you hear.

1. [✓] You have to see the old train station.

   [ ] You hafta see the old train station.

2. [ ] Travelers need to be careful of the environment.

   [ ] Travelers needta be careful of the environment.

3. [ ] He has to see the famous garden.

   [ ] He hasta see the famous garden.

4. [ ] Visitors ought to help the local economy.

   [ ] Visitors oughta help the local economy.

F. Work with a partner. Partner A says a sentence from Activity E. Partner B points to the correct sentence. Then partners switch roles.

G. Listen. Complete the conversations with the words you hear.

1. A: I'm tired. What should I do?

   B: You _____ take a nap.

2. A: The test is tomorrow.

   B: Yes. We _____ study!

3. A: I want to go to Easter Island.

   B: You _____ go soon.

4. A: Traveling is expensive.

   B: You _____ save some money.

Chant

GO ONLINE for the Chapter 8 Vocabulary and Grammar Chant

A. Here are some important structures and places in the world. Think of more examples. Then work with a group to answer the question.

Why should we take care of these places?

| Great Wall of China | pyramids of Egypt | Victoria Falls, Zambia |

B. Listen to the first part of the lecture. What is the speaker going to talk about? Circle the correct answer.

important sites at risk   *waterfalls and forests*   *the Great Wall of China*

C. Listen to the second part of the lecture. Match the places and the problems.

1. _____ a church in Peru   a. global warming (higher temperatures)

2. _____ a forest in Uganda   b. earthquakes

Listening Strategy

Listening for causes and effects

Speakers use certain words and phrases to connect causes and effects. Listen to the examples.

    cause   effect
*It's hot today, **so** we have to give more water to the plants.*

          cause   effect
***Because of** the earthquake last year, there is a lot of damage in the old part of town.*

    cause   effect
*A self-driving car **caused** an accident yesterday.*

    cause   effect
*It rained this morning. **As a result**, the streets are wet.*

GO ONLINE
for more
practice

D. Listen to parts of the lecture again. Complete the sentences with the cause-effect expressions from the box. You will use one expression twice.

as a result	because	caused	so

1. There were many earthquakes in the 1800s and the 1900s.

   _____As a result_____, the church was damaged.

2. And an earthquake in 2001 _____ even more damage.

3. Many sites are at risk right now _____ the earth is getting

   hotter.

4. The plants are dying. _____, the gorillas have to move to new

   places to find food.

5. We want to protect special places like these, _____ we must

   take care of them.

E. Listen to the lecture again. Then ask and answer the questions with a partner.

Partner A	Partner B
1. Why should we care about important sites?	2. What is one cause of problems at important sites?
3. What is another cause of problems at important sites?	4. What happened to a church in Peru?
5. What is happening to a forest in Uganda?	6. Who should we save these important sites for?

Discuss the Ideas

F. Work with a group. Discuss the list of places in Activity A and your own ideas.

Partner A	Partner B		Partner A	Partner B
Which place do you want to see?	I want to see	the Great Wall of China the pyramids of Egypt Victoria Falls	Why do you want to see it?	Because…

Speaking Task Describing an important place and explaining why we should protect it

Step 1 PREPARE

Pronunciation Skill

Reduction of *have to* and *has to*

🔊 When speakers use *have to* and *has to*, the *to* sometimes sounds like *ta*. Listen to the examples.

The *v* in *have to* sounds like *f* when you reduce it.

I **have to** see Easter Island. → I **hafta** see Easter Island.

They **have to** go now. → They **hafta** go now.

She **has to** buy a new car. → She **hasta** buy a new car.

He **has to** travel next week. → He **hasta** travel next week.

GO ONLINE
for more
practice

🔊 **A. Listen to the sentences. Check (✓) *same* if you hear the same sentence. Check (✓) *different* if the sentences are different.**

1. [✓] same   [ ] different

2. [ ] same   [ ] different

3. [ ] same   [ ] different

4. [ ] same   [ ] different

5. [ ] same   [ ] different

6. [ ] same   [ ] different

🔊 **B. Listen and repeat.**

1. We hafta go.

2. She hasta see this.

3. He hasta leave.

4. They hafta study.

5. I hafta wait.

6. She hasta come.

C. Listen. Complete each conversation with *have to* or *has to*.

1. A: What's the most important building in your town?

   B: Let me think… Oh, yeah. It's the old library. It's a beautiful building. You _____have to_____ see it!

2. A: Ana can't go with us to Easter Island this summer. It's too expensive for her. She _____ save money instead.

3. A: Is Tai in Mexico City?

   B: No. He's still here. He _____ get a new passport first.

4. A: We _____ be very careful here. There's a lot of traffic. I don't want to have an accident.

5. A: The city is going to tear down the old train station!

   B: Oh, no. That train station is beautiful. We _____ help save it!

6. A: In California, we visited an ancient forest. Some of the trees are 800 years old.

   B: Wow! I _____ see that!

GO ONLINE
to practice the conversations

D. Work with a partner. Practice the conversations in Activity C.

E. Work with a partner. Partner A asks a question. Partner B answers correctly. Then partners switch roles.

1. a. Why do we have to protect the island?   Soon. It's getting crowded.

   b. When does she have to visit the island?   The hotels are damaging the environment.

2. a. What do we have to see in your town?   Because they're beautiful.

   b. Why do we have to see the gardens?   You have to see the famous gardens.

3. a. Why does she have to bring a camera?   There are a lot of interesting things to see there.

   b. Does she have to bring a camera?   No, she doesn't. But she has to bring her phone.

4. a. What do we have to think about on your trip?   We have to think about protecting the environment.

   b. Why do we have to think about the environment?   Because we need to protect it.

5. a. Why does he have to see it now?   The ancient forest in California.

   b. What does he have to see now?   Because global warming is destroying the forest.

A. **Think of some famous sites and landmarks. Why is each one important? Why should people protect it? Take notes in the chart.**

Famous site/landmark	We should protect it because...

B. **Work with a partner. Describe each site or landmark you listed in Activity A. Explain why people should preserve it.**

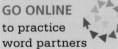
Speaking Skill

Expressing opinions and agreeing and disagreeing

🔊 Speakers use certain expressions to introduce opinions and to agree or disagree with opinions. Listen to the examples.

A: **In my opinion**, we have to protect the library.

B: **I agree.** / **I think** so, too.

C: **I disagree**. I **don't think** the library is as important as the train station.

A: **I think** travel should be educational.

B: **You're right**. We should always try to learn new things.

C: **I don't think so**. I think travel should be fun.

C. **Work with a partner. Partner A completes a sentence with an opinion expression. Partner B agrees or disagrees. Then partners switch roles.**

I agree	I disagree	You're right	I don't think so	I think so, too

1. _____. Global warming is/is not a problem.

2. _____. Learning a new language is/is not hard.

3. _____. We have to/don't have protect the environment.

4. _____. Exercise is/is not important.

5. _____. We need/don't need more parks in this town.

Speaking Task Describing an important place and explaining why we should protect it

1. With your group, choose a site or landmark from your notes in Step 2. Find or take a picture of the site or landmark. Describe it and explain why we should protect it. Organize your ideas in the chart.

What is the site or landmark?	
What does it look like?	
Why should we protect it?	

2. In your group, practice describing the site or landmark and giving your opinions on why we should protect it.

3. Work with another group. Close your books. Tell the other group about your site. Give as much information as you can. Show your picture. Listen to the other group's presentations. Ask questions and give opinions.

Step 3 REPORT

A. Choose one group's presentation. Write notes about it in the chart.

Site or landmark	Why we should protect it	My opinion

B. Share your notes. Which site or landmark is the most important? Why is it the most important?

Step 4 REFLECT

Checklist

Check (✓) the things you learned in Chapter 8.

- ○ I learned language for talking about important sites and landmarks.
- ○ I understood speakers asking for and giving specific details.
- ○ I described an important place and explained why we should protect it.

Discussion Question

Imagine your town or city does not protect an important site or landmark. What might happen?

- Use *be* + adjective + preposition
- Recognize promotional language
- Reduce prepositions after adjectives
- Listen to take notes with a T-chart
- Practice sentence stress
- Present a position in a debate

▲ VOCABULARY ▶ Oxford 2000 🔑 words to talk about adventure

Learn Words

🔊 **A. Label each picture with the correct word. Then listen and repeat the words and phrases.**

a challenge   a risk   an adventure   danger   exploring   heights   the dark   the environment

1.

ready for _____*a challenge*_____

2.

afraid of _____

3.

aware of _____

4.

used to _____

5.

excited about _____

6.

interested in _____

7.

not careful about _____

8.

not afraid of _____

Grammar Note

be + adjective + preposition

Speakers use *be* with adjectives and prepositions before nouns to describe attitudes and feelings about things. Listen to the examples.

> I**'m used to** *public transportation.*
>
> He**'s excited about** *the trip.*
>
> We**'re interested in** *a cave tour.*

To form the negative, speakers use *not* before the adjective.

> I**'m not afraid of** *risk.*

To ask questions, speakers use *am/is/are* before the subject. Listen to the examples.

> A: **Are** *you* **afraid of** *the dark?*   B: *No, I'm not.*
>
> A: *What* **is** *he* **interested in**?   B: *He's interested in music.*

B. Listen and repeat.

1. Raul is afraid of the dark.

2. Jun isn't aware of the environment.

3. I'm excited about adventure travel.

4. They're not interested in art.

5. She isn't afraid of high places.

6. We're ready for a challenge.

7. Paolo is used to heights.

8. Ana is interested in engineering.

C. Listen and repeat each question and answer.

Questions	Answers
1. What are you afraid of?	I'm afraid of heights.
2. Are you ready for a challenge?	Yes, I am. Let's go!
3. Is Raul used to heights?	Yes, he is. He's a mountain climber.
4. Why is Wei interested in bungee jumping?	He likes to jump from high places.
5. Are you afraid of the dark?	No, I'm not. I'm comfortable in the dark.
6. What are you interested in?	I'm interested in exploring Paris.

 D. Work with a partner. Partner A asks a question from Activity B. Partner B answers. Then partners switch roles.

Learn Phrases

🔊 **A. Match each phrase to the correct picture. Then listen and repeat.**

be aware of history and **other cultures**	not be aware of the environment and **cause damage**
explore tunnels under a city	not be prepared for **physical challenges**
go bungee jumping **off a bridge**	**take a risk** and succeed

1.

2.

3.

4.

5.

6.

B. Listen to the conversations. Match the phrases with the situations.

a. be aware of history and other cultures

b. explore tunnels under a city

c. go bungee jumping off a bridge

d. ~~not be aware of the environment and~~ ~~cause damage~~

e. not be prepared for physical challenges

f. take a risk and succeed

Situation 1: ___d___

Situation 2: _____

Situation 3: _____

Situation 4: _____

Situation 5: _____

Situation 6: _____

C. Work with a partner. Discuss your answers to the questions.

1. Do you want to go bungee jumping off a high bridge? Why or why not?

2. Do you want to explore tunnels under a city? Why or why not?

3. Do you like physical challenges? Why or why not?

4. Think of a time you took a risk and succeeded. What did you do? Why did you succeed?

> Do you want to go bungee jumping off a high bridge?

> No. I'm afraid of heights. How about you?

> Sure. It sounds like fun.

GO ONLINE for more practice

▲▲ LISTENING

CONVERSATION

A. Listen to the presentation. What is the purpose of the presentation? Circle the correct answer.

to describe a personal experience   *to teach a lesson*   *to sell something*

B. Listen to the presentation again. Match the details with the tours. There are two details for each tour.

a. You can go to the top of a mountain in Tanzania.

b. You can see the largest waterfall in the world.

~~c. You can explore tunnels.~~

d. You can see a cemetery.

e. You can see the border between Chile and Peru.

f. You can do this in a rainforest in Costa Rica.

1. Paris Underground: __c__ _____

2. Bungee Jumping around the World: _____ _____

3. Mountain Climbing Tour: _____ _____

Listening Strategy

Recognize promotional language

Speakers often use certain words to try to sell things. They use strong adjectives like *new*, *best*, and *exciting*. They use verbs that tell you to do something like *try*, *get*, and *buy*. Listen to the examples.

Get the **new** XPhone 538. It's **the best** XPhone ever! **Come** to your local XPhone shop today and **try** it.

GO ONLINE
for more practice

C. Listen to parts of the presentation again. Complete the promotional lines with the words from the box. You will use one word twice.

best	exciting	new	take	try

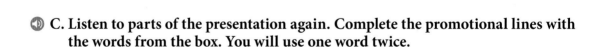

1. We have the _____ city exploration tour in the world, the Paris

   Underground Adventure.

2. For one of the most _____ vacations ever, _____ our

   _____ Mountain Climbing Tour.

3. So, _____ one of our adventure tours and be prepared for the

   _____ vacation you'll ever have!

Reducing prepositions after adjectives

🔊 When speakers use adjectives + *to* and *of*, they often reduce the preposition. Listen to the examples.

> **The *d* in *used to* sounds like *t* when you reduce it.**
> We're **used to** heights. → We're **useta** heights.
>
> Are you **afraid of** the dark? → Are you **afraida** the dark?
>
> I'm **aware of** the problem. → I'm **awarea** the problem.

🔊 **D. Listen to the sentences. Check (✓)** *same* **if you hear the same sentence. Check (✓)** *different* **if the sentences are different.**

1. [✓] same   [ ] different

2. [ ] same   [ ] different

3. [ ] same   [ ] different

4. [ ] same   [ ] different

5. [ ] same   [ ] different

6. [ ] same   [ ] different

🔊 **E. Listen. Complete the conversations with the words you hear.**

1. A: Why don't you want to go on the cave tour?
   B: I'm _____ atraid ot _____ the dark!

2. A: Those adventure tours are expensive!
   B: I know. I wasn't _____ the cost.

3. A: Are you staying home for a while?
   B: Yes. I'm _____ traveling.

4. A: I'm still not _____ the food here.
   B: I know, but you'll get used to it soon.

5. A: Travelers are leaving garbage on the beach.
   B: I know. They're not _____ the environment.

 F. Work with a partner. Practice the conversations in Activity E.

Chant

GO ONLINE
for the
Chapter 9
Vocabulary and
Grammar Chant

A. Look at the list of travel activities. Add two more travel activities to the list. Think about reasons people like to do these activities. Write your ideas in the chart. Then discuss your ideas with a partner.

Activities	People like to do this because...
bungee jumping exploring caves mountain climbing skydiving surfing _____ _____	

B. Listen to the first part of the lecture. What is the speaker going to do? Circle the correct answer.

give an opinion about an issue   *show two sides of an issue*   *explain the history of an issue*

C. Listen to the first part of the lecture again. Complete the definition of *extreme tourism.*

Extreme tourism is traveling to _____ places and doing

_____ activities.

Listening Strategy

Listening to take notes with a T-chart

It's a good idea to take notes when you are listening to an academic presentation. One way to take notes is with a T-chart. With a T-chart, you write ideas side by side. A T-chart helps you to see two sides of an issue. Listen to the speaker and study the T-chart.

Pro: Tear down the old train station.	Con: Don't tear down the old train station.
1. We need a better, new one. 2. We need more office buildings downtown.	1. It's an important, historic building. 2. More office buildings downtown will increase traffic.

GO ONLINE
for more
practice

D. Listen to the second part of the lecture. Complete the ideas in the T-chart with the words from the box.

accidents   bad   climbing and hiking   educational   emotional   important sites

Pro: Extreme tourism	Con: Extreme tourism
1. _____ benefits Example: people feel good when they do something challenging	1. dangerous Example: _____ such as skydiving in New Zealand
2. physical benefits Example: _____ make you stronger	2. emotional problems Example: people feel _____ if they cannot do something challenging
3. _____ benefits Example: people can learn about history and culture	3. bad for the environment Example: damage to _____ such as underground grave in Paris

E. Listen to the lecture again. Then ask and answer the questions with a partner.

Partner A	Partner B
1. What is extreme tourism?	2. What is one good thing about extreme tourism?
3. What is another good thing about extreme tourism?	4. What is one problem with extreme tourism?
5. What is another problem with extreme tourism?	6. What should people do if they want to go on an extreme trip?

Discuss the Ideas

F. Work with a group. Discuss your answers to the questions.

Do you want to go on an extreme trip? Why or why not?

Speaking Task Presenting a position in a debate

Step 1 PREPARE

Pronunciation Skill

Sentence stress

🔊 Speakers stress certain words in sentences. Usually, these words are nouns, main verbs, and adjectives. Listen to the examples.

> *This is* **Mia**.
>
> *She* **works** *here.*
>
> *It's* **beautiful***!*
>
> *We* **want** *to visit the* **old train** *station.*

Note: With compound nouns, speakers usually stress only the first noun; for example, *train*, not *station*.

GO ONLINE
for more
practice

🔊 **A. Listen to each sentence. Underline the stressed words.**

1. Surfing is dangerous.

2. It's a good idea.

3. He likes bungee jumping.

4. It's bad for the environment.

5. She's afraid of the dark.

6. I'm not prepared for danger.

🔊 **B. Listen and repeat the questions and answers. Pay attention to the stressed words.**

Questions	Answers
1. What are you interested in?	I'm interested in adventure travel.
2. What are you worried about?	I'm worried about the test.
3. What are you afraid of?	I'm afraid of flying.
4. Where do you want to go?	I want to go to Peru.
5. What are you used to?	I'm used to hard work.
6. What are you excited about?	I'm excited about the underground tunnels.

C. Work with a partner. Ask and answer the questions in Activity B.

 D. Listen. Complete the conversation with the stressed words from the box.

beach	crazy	dangerous	extreme	great	heights
mountain	Paris	prepared	relaxing	vacation	

A: What do you think of

_____extreme_____ tourism?

B: I think it's _____.

A: What do you mean?

B: Skydiving, bungee jumping,

_____ climbing…

That's not my idea of a fun

_____!

A: Why not?

B: Well, first of all, I'm not in good shape.

And I'm afraid of _____!

A: I see what you mean.

B: Extreme tourism is _____.

A: Well, especially for someone like you!

B: Right. I'm just not _____ for risk. It's not fun.

A: I get it. So, what's your idea of a _____ vacation?

B: I'm mostly interested in _____. My idea of a great vacation is doing nothing.

A: Then I guess you aren't going on the _____ Underground tour with me.

B: No. I think I'll go to the _____ instead.

GO ONLINE to practice the conversation

 E. Work with a partner. Practice the conversation in Activity D.

A. Work with a group. Think about the debate issue "Is extreme tourism a good idea?" Think of reasons for each side of the issue. Use the reasons from the lecture or your own ideas.

 B. Work with another group. Practice explaining both sides of the issue.

> Extreme tourism is a good idea because it helps people get fit. For example, exploring tunnels under a city is a good way to get exercise.

> Extreme tourism is not a good idea because it is bad for the environment. For example, exploring tunnels under a city can damage ancient structures.

Word Partners

avoid danger

be aware of danger

cause danger

lessen danger

recognize danger

GO ONLINE
to practice
word partners

Speaking Skill

Summarizing in a debate

In a debate, speakers often summarize—give a short explanation of—the reasons on the other side. They summarize a reason from the other side, and then they give a reason for their side. They connect the summary and their reason with a transition word such as *however* or *but*. Listen to the example.

summary of other side

The other side believes that extreme tourism is bad because it's dangerous. However, people can prepare for extreme tourism. That way, they can avoid accidents.

speaker's side

transition word

 C. Work with a partner. Discuss the issues in the chart. Summarize a side, use a transition word, and give the other side.

Issue	Pro side	Con side
Should you always buy the latest tech device?	It's important to know how to use technology.	It's too expensive.
Is exercise important?	Exercise keeps you fit.	Exercise doesn't help you lose weight.
Should we tear down old buildings?	New buildings are better for the environment.	Old buildings tell us about the history of a place.

Speaking Task
Presenting a position in a debate

1. With your group, choose a side of the issue "Is extreme tourism a good idea?" To help you choose, think about these questions: Which side do you believe in the most? Which side has the strongest reasons and examples? Which side is the easiest to explain? Organize your ideas in the chart.

Your side: Extreme tourism is / is not a good idea.

Reason 1: _____
    Examples: _____
    _____

Reason 2: _____
    Examples: _____
    _____

Reason 3: _____
    Examples: _____
    _____

2. In your group, practice presenting your side of the issue.

3. Work with a group on the other side. Debate the issue by taking turns presenting reasons and examples.

Step 3 REPORT

Practice presenting the *opposite* side of the issue, not the side you presented in the debate. Then answer the questions.

Which side did you believe in before? Which side do you believe in now? Did your opinion change? Why or why not?

Step 4 REFLECT

Checklist

Check (✓) the things you learned in Chapter 9.

○ I learned language for talking about about adventure travel.

○ I understood speakers using promotional language.

○ I presented a side in a debate on extreme tourism.

Discussion Question

Why do some people like to do dangerous things?

Extend Your Skills

Look at the word bank for Unit 3. Check (✓) the words you know. Circle the words you want to learn better.

OXFORD 2000 🔑

Adjectives	Nouns		Verbs
different	adventure	environment	cause
extreme	animal	forest	explore
good	art	garden	have
local	bridge	height	help
natural	building	language	learn
old	challenge	part	look
other	church	past	make
physical	city	picture	protect
	culture	plant	shop
	damage	risk	speak
	danger	structure	stay
	dark	town	take
	disaster	tunnel	tear
	dish	type	tell
	economy	wonder	visit

PRACTICE WITH THE OXFORD 2000 🔑

A. Use the chart. Match adjectives with nouns.

1. _physical challenge_   2. _____

3. _____   4. _____

5. _____   6. _____

B. Use the chart. Match verbs with nouns.

1. _cause damage_   2. _____

3. _____   4. _____

5. _____   6. _____

C. Use the chart. Match verbs with adjective noun partners.

1. _protect old buildings_   2. _____

3. _____   4. _____

5. _____   6. _____

This is a list of the 2000 most important and useful words to learn at this stage in your language learning. These words have been carefully chosen by a group of language experts and experienced teachers, who have judged the words to be important and useful for three reasons.

- Words that are used very **frequently** (= very often) in English are included in this list. Frequency information has been gathered from the American English section of the Oxford English Corpus, which is a collection of written and spoken texts containing over 2 billion words.

- The keywords are frequent across a **range** of different types of text. This means that the keywords are often used in a variety of contexts, not just in newspapers or in scientific articles for example.

- The list includes some important words which are very **familiar** to most users of English, even though they are not used very frequently. These include, for example, words which are useful for explaining what you mean when you do not know the exact word for something.

Names of people, places, etc. beginning with a capital letter are not included in the list of 2000 keywords. Keywords which are not included in the list are numbers, days of the week, and the months of the year.

A

a, an *indefinite article*
ability *n.*
able *adj.*
about *adv., prep.*
above *prep., adv.*
absolutely *adv.*
academic *adj.*
accept *v.*
acceptable *adj.*
accident *n.*
  by accident
according to *prep.*
account *n.*
accurate *adj.*
accuse *v.*
achieve *v.*
achievement *n.*
acid *n.*
across *adv., prep.*
act *n., v.*
action *n.*
active *adj.*
activity *n.*
actor, actress *n.*
actual *adj.*
actually *adv.*
add *v.*
address *n.*
admire *v.*
admit *v.*
adult *n.*
advanced *adj.*
advantage *n.*
adventure *n.*
advertisement *n.*
advice *n.*

advise *v.*
affect *v.*
afford *v.*
afraid *adj.*
after *prep., conj., adv.*
afternoon *n.*
afterward *adv.*
again *adv.*
against *prep.*
age *n.*
  aged *adj.*
ago *adv.*
agree *v.*
agreement *n.*
ahead *adv.*
aim *n., v.*
air *n.*
airplane *n.*
airport *n.*
alarm *n.*
alcohol *n.*
alcoholic *adj.*
alive *adj.*
all *adj., pron., adv.*
allow *v.*
all right *adj., adv.,*
  exclamation
almost *adv.*
alone *adj., adv.*
along *prep., adv.*
alphabet *n.*
already *adv.*
also *adv.*
although *conj.*
always *adv.*
among *prep.*
amount *n.*

amuse *v.*
analyze *v.*
analysis *n.*
ancient *adj.*
and *conj.*
anger *n.*
angle *n.*
angry *adj.*
animal *n.*
announce *v.*
another *adj., pron.*
answer *n., v.*
any *adj., pron., adv.*
anymore *(also* any more*)*
  adv.
anyone *(also* anybody*)*
  pron.
anything *pron.*
anyway *adv.*
anywhere *adv.*
apart *adv.*
apartment *n.*
apparently *adv.*
appear *v.*
appearance *n.*
apple *n.*
apply *v.*
appointment *n.*
appreciate *v.*
appropriate *adj.*
approve *v.*
area *n.*
argue *v.*
argument *n.*
arm *n.*
army *n.*
around *adv., prep.*

arrange *v.*
arrangement *n.*
arrest *v.*
arrive *v.*
arrow *n.*
art *n.*
article *n.*
artificial *adj.*
artist *n.*
artistic *adj.*
as *prep., conj.*
ashamed *adj.*
ask *v.*
asleep *adj.*
at *prep.*
atmosphere *n.*
atom *n.*
attach *v.*
attack *n., v.*
attention *n.*
attitude *n.*
attract *v.*
attractive *adj.*
aunt *n.*
authority *n.*
available *adj.*
average *adj., n.*
avoid *v.*
awake *adj.*
aware *adj.*
away *adv.*

B

baby *n.*
back *n., adj., adv.*
backward *adv.*
bad *adj.*

badly *adv.*
bag *n.*
bake *v.*
balance *n.*
ball *n.*
band *n.*
bank *n.*
bar *n.*
base *n., v.*
baseball *n.*
basic *adj.*
basis *n.*
bath *n.*
bathroom *n.*
be *v.*
beach *n.*
bear *v.*
beard *n.*
beat *v.*
beautiful *adj.*
beauty *n.*
because *conj.*
become *v.*
bed *n.*
bedroom *n.*
beer *n.*
before *prep., conj., adv.*
begin *v.*
beginning *n.*
behave *v.*
behavior *n.*
behind *prep., adv.*
belief *n.*
believe *v.*
bell *n.*
belong *v.*
below *prep., adv.*
belt *n.*
bend *v.*
benefit *n.*
beside *prep.*
best *adj., adv., n.*
better *adj., adv.*
between *prep., adv.*
beyond *prep., adv.*
bicycle *n.*
big *adj.*
bill *n.*
bird *n.*
birth *n.*
birthday *n.*
bite *v.*
bitter *adj.*
black *adj.*
blame *v.*
block *n.*
blood *n.*
blow *v., n.*
blue *adj., n.*

board *n.*
boat *n.*
body *n.*
boil *v.*
bomb *n., v.*
bone *n.*
book *n.*
boot *n.*
border *n.*
bored *adj.*
boring *adj.*
born: be born *v.*
borrow *v.*
boss *n.*
both *adj., pron.*
bother *v.*
bottle *n.*
bottom *n.*
bowl *n.*
box *n.*
boy *n.*
boyfriend *n.*
brain *n.*
branch *n.*
brave *adj.*
bread *n.*
break *v.*
breakfast *n.*
breath *n.*
breathe *v.*
brick *n.*
bridge *n.*
brief *adj.*
bright *adj.*
bring *v.*
broken *adj.*
brother *n.*
brown *adj., n.*
brush *n., v.*
bubble *n.*
build *v.*
building *n.*
bullet *n.*
burn *v.*
burst *v.*
bury *v.*
bus *n.*
bush *n.*
business *n.*
busy *adj.*
but *conj.*
butter *n.*
button *n.*
buy *v.*
by *prep.*
bye *exclamation*

C

cabinet *n.*

cake *n.*
calculate *v.*
call *v., n.*
calm *adj.*
camera *n.*
camp *n., v.*
can *modal v., n.*
cancel *v.*
candy *n.*
capable *adj.*
capital *n.*
car *n.*
card *n.*
care *n., v.*
    take care of
    care for
career *n.*
careful *adj.*
carefully *adv.*
careless *adj.*
carelessly *adv.*
carry *v.*
case *n.*
    in case (of)
cash *n.*
cat *n.*
catch *v.*
cause *n., v.*
CD *n.*
ceiling *n.*
celebrate *v.*
cell *n.*
cell phone *n.*
cent *n.*
center *n.*
centimeter *n.*
central *adj.*
century *n.*
ceremony *n.*
certain *adj.*
certainly *adv.*
chain *n., v.*
chair *n.*
challenge *n.*
chance *n.*
change *v., n.*
character *n.*
characteristic *n.*
charge *n., v.*
charity *n.*
chase *v., n.*
cheap *adj.*
cheat *v.*
check *v., n.*
cheek *n.*
cheese *n.*
chemical *adj., n.*
chemistry *n.*
chest *n.*

chicken *n.*
chief *adj., n.*
child *n.*
childhood *n.*
chin *n.*
chocolate *n.*
choice *n.*
choose *v.*
church *n.*
cigarette *n.*
circle *n.*
citizen *n.*
city *n.*
class *n.*
clean *adj., v.*
clear *adj., v.*
clearly *adv.*
climate *n.*
climb *v.*
clock *n.*
close /kloʊs/ *adj., adv.*
close /kloʊz/ *v.*
closed *adj.*
cloth *n.*
clothes *n.*
clothing *n.*
cloud *n.*
club *n.*
coast *n.*
coat *n.*
coffee *n.*
coin *n.*
cold *adj., n.*
collect *v.*
collection *n.*
college *n.*
color *n., v.*
column *n.*
combination *n.*
combine *v.*
come *v.*
comfortable *adj.*
command *n.*
comment *n., v.*
common *adj.*
communicate *v.*
communication *n.*
community *n.*
company *n.*
compare *v.*
comparison *n.*
competition *n.*
complain *v.*
complaint *n.*
complete *adj.*
completely *adv.*
complicated *adj.*
computer *n.*
concentrate *v.*

concert *n.*
conclusion *n.*
condition *n.*
confidence *n.*
confident *adj.*
confuse *v.*
confused *adj.*
connect *v.*
connection *n.*
conscious *adj.*
consider *v.*
consist *v.*
constant *adj.*
contact *n., v.*
contain *v.*
container *n.*
continent *n.*
continue *v.*
continuous *adj.*
contract *n.*
contrast *n.*
contribute *v.*
control *n., v.*
convenient *adj.*
conversation *n.*
convince *v.*
cook *v.*
cookie *n.*
cooking *n.*
cool *adj.*
copy *n., v.*
corner *n.*
correct *adj., v.*
correctly *adv.*
cost *n., v.*
cotton *n.*
cough *v.*
could *modal v.*
count *v.*
country *n*
county *n.*
couple *n.*
course *n.*
    of course
court *n.*
cousin *n.*
cover *v., n.*
covering *n.*
cow *n.*
crack *v.*
crash *n., v.*
crazy *adj.*
cream *n., adj.*
create *v.*
credit card *n.*
crime *n.*
criminal *adj., n.*
crisis *n.*
criticism *n.*

criticize *v.*
cross *v.*
crowd *n.*
cruel *adj.*
crush *v.*
cry *v.*
culture *n.*
cup *n.*
curly *adj.*
curve *n.*
curved *adj.*
custom *n.*
customer *n.*
cut *v., n.*

D

dad *n.*
damage *n., v.*
dance *n., v.*
dancer *n.*
danger *n.*
dangerous *adj.*
dark *adj., n.*
date *n.*
daughter *n.*
day *n.*
dead *adj.*
deal *v.*
dear *adj.*
death *n.*
debt *n.*
decide *v.*
decision *n.*
decorate *v.*
deep *adj.*
deeply *adv.*
defeat *v.*
definite *adj.*
definitely *adv.*
definition *n*
degree *n.*
deliberately *adv.*
deliver *v.*
demand *n., v.*
dentist *n.*
deny *v.*
department *n.*
depend *v.*
depression *n.*
describe *v.*
description *n.*
desert *n.*
deserve *v.*
design *n., v.*
desk *n.*
despite *prep.*
destroy *v.*
detail *n.*
    in detail

determination *n.*
determined *adj.*
develop *v.*
development *n.*
device *n.*
diagram *n.*
dictionary *n.*
die *v.*
difference *n.*
different *adj.*
difficult *adj.*
difficulty *n.*
dig *v.*
dinner *n.*
direct *adj., adv., v.*
direction *n.*
directly *adv.*
dirt *n.*
dirty *adj.*
disadvantage *n.*
disagree *v.*
disagreement *n.*
disappear *v.*
disappoint *v.*
disaster *n.*
discover *v.*
discuss *v.*
discussion *n.*
disease *n.*
disgusting *adj.*
dish *n.*
dishonest *adj.*
disk *n.*
distance *n.*
distant *adj.*
disturb *v.*
divide *v.*
division *n.*
divorce *n., v.*
do *v., auxiliary v.*
doctor *n. (abbr.* Dr.*)*
document *n.*
dog *n.*
dollar *n.*
door *n.*
dot *n.*
double *adj.*
doubt *n.*
down *adv., prep.*
downstairs *adv., adj.*
downward *adv.*
draw *v.*
drawer *n.*
drawing *n*
dream *n., v.*
dress *n., v.*
drink *n., v.*
drive *v., n.*
driver *n.*

drop *v., n.*
drug *n.*
dry *adj., v.*
during *prep.*
dust *n.*
duty *n.*
DVD *n.*

E

each *adj., pron.*
each other *pron.*
ear *n.*
early *adj., adv.*
earn *v.*
earth *n.*
easily *adv.*
east *n., adj., adv.*
eastern *adj.*
easy *adj.*
eat *v.*
economic *adj.*
economy *n.*
edge *n.*
educate *v.*
education *n.*
effect *n.*
effort *n.*
e.g. *abbr.*
egg *n.*
either *adj., pron., adv.*
election *n.*
electric *adj.*
electrical *adj.*
electricity *n.*
electronic *adj.*
else *adv.*
e-mail *(also* email*) n., v.*
embarrass *v.*
embarrassed *adj.*
emergency *n.*
emotion *n.*
employ *v*
employment *n.*
empty *adj.*
encourage *v.*
end *n., v.*
    in the end
enemy *n.*
energy *n.*
engine *n.*
enjoy *v.*
enjoyable *adj.*
enjoyment *n.*
enough *adj., pron., adv.*
enter *v.*
entertain *v.*
entertainment *n.*
enthusiasm *n.*
enthusiastic *adj.*

entrance *n.*
environment *n.*
equal *adj.*
equipment *n.*
error *n.*
escape *v.*
especially *adv.*
essential *adj.*
etc. *abbr.*
even *adv.*
evening *n.*
event *n.*
ever *adv.*
every *adj.*
everybody *pron.*
everyone *pron.*
everything *pron.*
everywhere *adv.*
evidence *n.*
evil *adj.*
exact *adj.*
exactly *adv.*
exaggerate *v.*
exam *n.*
examination *n.*
examine *v.*
example *n.*
excellent *adj.*
except *prep.*
exchange *v., n.*
excited *adj.*
excitement *n.*
exciting *adj.*
excuse *n., v.*
exercise *n.*
exist *v.*
exit *n.*
expect *v.*
expensive *adj.*
experience *n., v.*
experiment *n.*
expert *n.*
explain *v.*
explanation *n.*
explode *v.*
explore *v.*
explosion *n.*
expression *n.*
extra *adj., adv.*
extreme *adj.*
extremely *adv.*
eye *n.*

F
face *n., v.*
fact *n.*
factory *n.*
fail *v.*
failure *n.*

fair *adj.*
fall *v., n.*
false *adj.*
familiar *adj.*
family *n.*
famous *adj.*
far *adv., adj.*
farm *n.*
farmer *n.*
fashion *n.*
fashionable *adj.*
fast *adj., adv.*
fasten *v.*
fat *adj., n.*
father *n.*
fault *n.*
favor *n.*
    in favor
favorite *adj., n.*
fear *n., v.*
feather *n.*
feature *n.*
feed *v.*
feel *v.*
feeling *n.*
female *adj.*
fence *n.*
festival *n.*
few *adj., pron.*
    a few
field *n.*
fight *v., n.*
figure *n.*
file *n.*
fill *v.*
film *n.*
final *adj.*
finally *adv.*
financial *adj.*
find *v.*
    find out sth
fine *adj.*
finger *n.*
finish *v.*
fire *n., v.*
firm *n., adj.*
firmly *adv.*
first *adj., adv., n.*
    at first
fish *n.*
fit *v., adj.*
fix *v.*
fixed *adj.*
flag *n.*
flame *n.*
flash *v.*
flat *adj.*
flavor *n.*
flight *n.*

float *v.*
flood *n.*
floor *n.*
flour *n.*
flow *v.*
flower *n.*
fly *v.*
fold *v.*
follow *v.*
food *n.*
foot *n.*
football *n.*
for *prep.*
force *n., v.*
foreign *adj.*
forest *n.*
forever *adv.*
forget *v.*
forgive *v.*
fork *n.*
form *n., v.*
formal *adj.*
forward *adv.*
frame *n.*
free *adj., v., adv.*
freedom *n.*
freeze *v.*
fresh *adj.*
friend *n.*
friendly *adj.*
friendship *n.*
frighten *v.*
from *prep.*
front *n., adj.*
    in front
frozen *adj.*
fruit *n.*
fry *v.*
fuel *n.*
full *adj.*
fully *adv.*
fun *n., adj.*
funny *adj.*
fur *n.*
furniture *n.*
further *adj., adv.*
future *n., adj.*

G
gain *v.*
gallon *n.*
game *n.*
garbage *n.*
garden *n.*
gas *n.*
gate *n.*
general *adj.*
    in general
generally *adv.*

generous *adj.*
gentle *adj.*
gently *adv.*
gentleman *n.*
get *v.*
gift *n.*
girl *n.*
girlfriend *n.*
give *v.*
glass *n.*
glasses *n.*
global *adj.*
glove *n.*
go *v.*
goal *n.*
god *n.*
gold *n., adj.*
good *adj., n.*
goodbye *exclamation*
goods *n.*
govern *v.*
government *n.*
grade *n., v.*
grain *n.*
gram *n.*
grammar *n.*
grandchild *n.*
grandfather *n.*
grandmother *n.*
grandparent *n.*
grass *n.*
grateful *adj.*
gray *adj., n.*
great *adj.*
green *adj., n.*
groceries *n.*
ground *n.*
group *n.*
grow *v.*
growth *n.*
guard *n., v.*
guess *v.*
guest *n.*
guide *n.*
guilty *adj.*
gun *n.*

H
habit *n.*
hair *n.*
half *n., adj., pron., adv.*
hall *n.*
hammer *n.*
hand *n.*
handle *v., n.*
hang *v.*
happen *v.*
happiness *n.*
happy *adj.*

hard *adj., adv.*
hardly *adv.*
harm *n., v.*
harmful *adj.*
hat *n.*
hate *v., n.*
have *v.*
　　have to *modal v.*
he *pron.*
head *n.*
health *n.*
healthy *adj.*
hear *v.*
heart *n.*
heat *n., v.*
heavy *adj.*
height *n.*
hello *exclamation*
help *v., n.*
helpful *adj.*
her *pron., adj.*
here *adv.*
hers *pron.*
herself *pron.*
hide *v.*
high *adj., adv.*
highly *adv.*
high school *n.*
highway *n.*
hill *n.*
him *pron.*
himself *pron.*
hire *v.*
his *adj., pron.*
history *n.*
hit *v., n.*
hold *v., n.*
hole *n.*
holiday *n.*
home *n., adv..*
honest *adj.*
hook *n.*
hope *v., n.*
horn *n.*
horse *n.*
hospital *n.*
hot *adj.*
hotel *n.*
hour *n.*
house *n.*
how *adv.*
however *adv.*
huge *adj.*
human *adj., n.*
humor *n.*
hungry *adj.*
hunt *v.*
hurry *v., n.*
hurt *v.*

husband *n.*

I

I *pron.*
ice *n.*
idea *n.*
identify *v.*
if *conj.*
ignore *v.*
illegal *adj.*
illegally *adv.*
illness *n.*
image *n.*
imagination *n.*
imagine *v.*
immediate *adj.*
immediately *adv.*
impatient *adj.*
importance *n.*
important *adj.*
impossible *adj.*
impress *v.*
impression *n.*
improve *v.*
improvement *n.*
in *prep., adv.*
inch *n.*
include *v.*
including *prep.*
increase *v., n.*
indeed *adv.*
independent *adj.*
individual *adj.*
industry *n.*
infection *n.*
influence *n.*
inform *v.*
informal *adj.*
information *n.*
injure *v.*
injury *n.*
insect *n.*
inside *prep., adv., n., adj.*
instead *adv., prep.*
instruction *n.*
instrument *n.*
insult *v., n.*
intelligent *adj.*
intend *v.*
intention *n.*
interest *n., v.*
interested *adj.*
interesting *adj.*
international *adj.*
Internet *n.*
interrupt *v.*
interview *n.*
into *prep.*
introduce *v.*

introduction *n.*
invent *v.*
investigate *v.*
invitation *n.*
invite *v.*
involve *v.*
iron *n.*
island *n.*
issue *n.*
it *pron.*
item *n.*
its *adj.*
itself *pron.*

J

jacket *n.*
jeans *n.*
jewelry *n.*
job *n.*
join *v.*
joke *n., v.*
judge *n., v.*
judgment *(also*
　　judgement) *n.*
juice *n.*
jump *v.*
just *adv.*

K

keep *v.*
key *n.*
kick *v., n.*
kid *n., v.*
kill *v.*
kilogram *(also* kilo) *n.*
kilometer *n.*
kind *n., adj.*
kindness *n.*
king *n.*
kiss *v., n.*
kitchen *n.*
knee *n.*
knife *n.*
knock *v., n.*
knot *n.*
know *v.*
knowledge *n.*

L

lack *n.*
lady *n.*
lake *n.*
lamp *n.*
land *n., v.*
language *n.*
large *adj.*
last *adj., adv., n., v.*
late *adj., adv.*
later *adv.*

laugh *v.*
laundry *n.*
law *n.*
lawyer *n.*
lay *v.*
layer *n.*
lazy *adj.*
lead /lid/ *v.*
leader *n.*
leaf *n.*
lean *v.*
learn *v.*
least *adj., pron., adv.*
　　at least
leather *n.*
leave *v.*
left *adj., adv., n.*
leg *n.*
legal *adj.*
legally *adv.*
lemon *n.*
lend *v.*
length *n.*
less *adj., pron., adv.*
lesson *n.*
let *v.*
letter *n.*
level *n.*
library *n.*
lid *n.*
lie *v., n.*
life *n.*
lift *v.*
light *n., adj., v.*
lightly *adv.*
like *prep., v., conj.*
likely *adj.*
limit *n., v.*
line *n.*
lip *n.*
liquid *n., adj.*
list *n., v.*
listen *v.*
liter *n.*
literature *n.*
little *adj., pron., adv.*
a little
live /lɪv/ *v.*
living *adj.*
load *n., v.*
loan *n.*
local *adj.*
lock *v., n.*
lonely *adj.*
long *adj., adv.*
look *v., n.*
loose *adj.*
lose *v.*
loss *n.*

lost *adj.*
lot *pron., adv.*
   a lot (of)
   lots (of)
loud *adj.*
loudly *adv.*
love *n., v.*
low *adj., adv.*
luck *n.*
lucky *adj.*
lump *n.*
lunch *n.*

M
machine *n.*
magazine *n.*
magic *n., adj.*
mail *n., v.*
main *adj.*
mainly *adv.*
make *v.*
male *adj., n.*
man *n.*
manage *v.*
manager *n.*
many *adj., pron.*
map *n.*
mark *n., v.*
market *n.*
marriage *n.*
married *adj.*
marry *v.*
match *n., v.*
material *n.*
math *n.*
mathematics *n.*
matter *n., v.*
may *modal v.*
maybe *adv.*
me *pron.*
meal *n.*
mean *v.*
meaning *n.*
measure *v., n.*
measurement *n.*
meat *n.*
medical *adj.*
medicine *n.*
medium *adj.*
meet *v.*
meeting *n.*
melt *v.*
member *n.*
memory *n.*
mental *adj.*
mention *v.*
mess *n.*
message *n.*
messy *adj.*

metal *n.*
method *n.*
meter *n.*
middle *n., adj.*
midnight *n.*
might *modal v.*
mile *n.*
milk *n.*
mind *n., v.*
mine *pron.*
minute *n.*
mirror *n.*
Miss *n.*
miss *v.*
missing *adj.*
mistake *n.*
mix *v.*
mixture *n.*
model *n.*
modern *adj.*
mom *n.*
moment *n.*
money *n.*
month *n.*
mood *n.*
moon *n.*
moral *adj.*
morally *adv.*
more *adj., pron., adv.*
morning *n.*
most *adj., pron., adv.*
mostly *adv.*
mother *n.*
motorcycle *n.*
mountain *n.*
mouse *n.*
mouth *n.*
move *v., n.*
movement *n.*
movie *n.*
Mr. *abbr.*
Mrs. *abbr.*
Ms. *abbr.*
much *adj., pron., adv.*
mud *n.*
multiply *v.*
murder *n., v.*
muscle *n.*
museum *n.*
music *n.*
musical *adj.*
musician *n.*
must *modal v.*
my *adj.*
myself *pron.*
mysterious *adj.*

N
nail *n.*

name *n., v.*
narrow *adj.*
nation *n.*
national *adj.*
natural *adj.*
nature *n.*
navy *n.*
near *adj., adv., prep.*
nearby *adj., adv.*
nearly *adv.*
neat *adj.*
neatly *adv.*
necessary *adj.*
neck *n.*
need *v., n.*
needle *n.*
negative *adj.*
neighbor *n.*
neither *adj., pron., adv.*
nerve *n.*
nervous *adj.*
net *n.*
never *adv.*
new *adj.*
news *n.*
newspaper *n.*
next *adj., adv., n.*
nice *adj.*
night *n.*
no *exclamation, adj.*
nobody *pron.*
noise *n.*
noisy *adj.*
noisily *adv.*
none *pron.*
nonsense *n.*
no one *pron.*
nor *conj.*
normal *adj.*
normally *adv.*
north *n., adj., adv.*
northern *adj.*
nose *n.*
not *adv.*
note *n.*
nothing *pron.*
notice *v.*
novel *n.*
now *adv.*
nowhere *adv.*
nuclear *adj.*
number (*abbr.* No., no.) *n.*
nurse *n.*
nut *n.*

O
object *n.*
obtain *v.*
obvious *adj.*

occasion *n.*
occur *v.*
ocean *n.*
o'clock *adv.*
odd *adj.*
of *prep.*
off *adv., prep.*
offense *n.*
offer *v., n.*
office *n.*
officer *n.*
official *adj., n.*
officially *adv.*
often *adv.*
oh *exclamation*
oil *n.*
OK (*also* okay)
   exclamation, adj., adv.
old *adj.*
old-fashioned *adj.*
on *prep., adv.*
once *adv., conj.*
one *number, adj., pron.*
onion *n.*
only *adj., adv.*
onto *prep.*
open *adj., v..*
operate *v.*
operation *n.*
opinion *n.*
opportunity *n.*
opposite *adj., adv., n., prep.*
or *conj.*
orange *n., adj.*
order *n., v.*
ordinary *adj.*
organization *n.*
organize *v.*
organized *adj.*
original *adj., n.*
other *adj., pron.*
otherwise *adv.*
ought to *modal v.*
ounce *n.*
our *adj.*
ours *pron.*
ourselves *pron.*
out *adj., adv.*
out of *prep.*
outside *n., adj., prep., adv.*
oven *n.*
over *adv., prep.*
owe *v.*
own *adj., pron., v.*
owner *n.*

P
pack *v., n.*
package *n.*

page *n.*
pain *n.*
painful *adj.*
paint *n., v.*
painter *n.*
painting *n.*
pair *n.*
pale *adj.*
pan *n.*
pants *n.*
paper *n.*
parent *n.*
park *n., v.*
part *n.*
   take part (in)
particular *adj.*
particularly *adv.*
partly *adv.*
partner *n.*
party *n.*
pass *v.*
passage *n.*
passenger *n.*
passport *n.*
past *adj., n., prep., adv.*
path *n.*
patient *n., adj.*
pattern *n.*
pause *v.*
pay *v., n.*
payment *n.*
peace *n.*
peaceful *adj.*
pen *n.*
pencil *n.*
people *n.*
perfect *adj.*
perform *v.*
performance *n.*
perhaps *adv.*
period *n.*
permanent *adj.*
permission *n.*
person *n.*
personal *adj.*
personality *n.*
persuade *v.*
pet *n.*
phone *n.*
photo *n.*
photograph *n.*
phrase *n.*
physical *adj.*
physically *adv.*
piano *n.*
pick *v.*
   pick sth up
picture *n.*
piece *n.*

pig *n.*
pile *n.*
pilot *n.*
pin *n.*
pink *adj., n.*
pint *n.*
pipe *n.*
place *n., v.*
   take place
plain *adj.*
plan *n., v.*
plane *n.*
planet *n.*
plant *n., v.*
plastic *n.*
plate *n.*
play *v., n.*
player *n.*
pleasant *adj.*
please *exclamation, v.*
pleased *adj.*
pleasure *n.*
plenty *pron.*
pocket *n.*
poem *n.*
poetry *n.*
point *n., v.*
pointed *adj.*
poison *n., v.*
poisonous *adj.*
police *n.*
polite *adj.*
politely *adv.*
political *adj.*
politician *n.*
politics *n.*
pollution *n.*
pool *n.*
poor *adj.*
popular *adj.*
port *n.*
position *n.*
positive *adj.*
possibility *n.*
possible *adj.*
possibly *adv.*
post *n.*
pot *n.*
potato *n.*
pound *n.*
pour *v.*
powder *n.*
power *n.*
powerful *adj.*
practical *adj.*
practice *n., v.*
prayer *n.*
prefer *v.*
pregnant *adj.*

preparation *n.*
prepare *v.*
present *adj., n., v.*
president *n.*
press *n., v.*
pressure *n.*
pretend *v.*
pretty *adv., adj.*
prevent *v.*
previous *adj.*
price *n.*
priest *n.*
principal *n.*
print *v.*
priority *n.*
prison *n.*
prisoner *n.*
private *adj.*
prize *n.*
probable *adj.*
probably *adv.*
problem *n.*
process *n.*
produce *v.*
product *n.*
production *n.*
professional *adj.*
profit *n.*
program *n.*
progress *n.*
project *n.*
promise *v., n.*
pronunciation *n.*
proof *n.*
proper *adj.*
property *n.*
protect *v.*
protection *n.*
protest *n.*
proud *adj.*
prove *v.*
provide *v.*
public *adj., n.*
   publicly *adv.*
publish *v.*
pull *v.*
punish *v.*
punishment *n.*
pure *adj.*
purple *adj., n.*
purpose *n.*
   on purpose
push *v., n.*
put *v.*

Q

quality *n.*
quantity *n.*
quarter *n.*

queen *n.*
question *n., v.*
quick *adj.*
quickly *adv.*
quiet *adj.*
quietly *adv.*
quite *adv.*

R

race *n., v.*
radio *n.*
railroad *n.*
rain *n., v.*
raise *v.*
rare *adj.*
rarely *adv.*
rate *n.*
rather *adv.*
reach *v.*
reaction *n.*
read *v.*
ready *adj.*
real *adj.*
reality *n.*
realize *v.*
really *adv.*
reason *n.*
reasonable *adj.*
receive *v.*
recent *adj.*
recently *adv.*
recognize *v.*
recommend *v.*
record *n., v.*
recover *v.*
red *adj., n.*
reduce *v.*
refer to *v.*
refuse *v.*
region *n.*
regular *adj.*
regularly *adv.*
relation *n.*
relationship *n.*
relax *v.*
relaxed *adj.*
release *v.*
relevant *adj.*
relief *n.*
religion *n.*
religious *adj.*
rely *v.*
remain *v.*
remark *n.*
remember *v.*
remind *v.*
remove *v.*
rent *n., v.*
repair *v., n.*

repeat *v.*
replace *v.*
reply *n., v.*
report *v., n.*
reporter *n.*
represent *v.*
request *n., v.*
require *v.*
rescue *v.*
research *n., v.*
reservation *n.*
respect *n., v.*
responsibility *n.*
responsible *adj.*
rest *n., v.*
restaurant *n.*
result *n., v.*
return *v., n.*
rice *n.*
rich *adj.*
rid *v.*: get rid of
ride *v., n.*
right *adj., adv., n.*
ring *n., v.*
rise *n., v.*
risk *n., v.*
river *n.*
road *n.*
rob *v.*
rock *n.*
role *n.*
roll *n., v.*
romantic *adj.*
roof *n.*
room *n.*
root *n.*
rope *n.*
rough *adj.*
round *adj.*
route *n.*
row *n.*
royal *adj.*
rub *v.*
rubber *n.*
rude *adj.*
   rudely *adv.*
ruin *v.*
rule *n., v.*
run *v., n.*
rush *v.*

S
sad *adj.*
sadness *n.*
safe *adj.*
safely *adv.*
safety *n.*
sail *v.*
salad *n.*

sale *n.*
salt *n.*
same *adj., pron.*
sand *n.*
satisfaction *n.*
satisfied *adj.*
sauce *n.*
save *v.*
say *v.*
scale *n.*
scare *v.*
scared *adj.*
scary *adj.*
schedule *n.*
school *n.*
science *n.*
scientific *adj.*
scientist *n.*
scissors *n.*
score *n., v.*
scratch *v., n.*
screen *n.*
search *n., v.*
season *n.*
seat *n.*
second *adj., adv., n.*
secret *adj., n.*
secretary *n.*
secretly *adv.*
section *n.*
see *v.*
seed *n.*
seem *v.*
sell *v.*
send *v.*
senior *adj.*
sense *n.*
sensible *adj.*
sensitive *adj.*
sentence n.
separate *adj., v.*
separately *adv.*
series *n.*
serious *adj.*
serve *v.*
service *n.*
set *n., v.*
settle *v.*
several *adj., pron.*
sew *v.*
sex *n.*
sexual *adj.*
shade *n.*
shadow *n.*
shake *v.*
shame *n.*
shape *n., v.*
   shaped *adj.*
share *v., n.*

sharp *adj.*
she *pron.*
sheep *n.*
sheet *n.*
shelf *n.*
shell *n.*
shine *v.*
shiny *adj.*
ship *n.*
shirt *n.*
shock *n., v.*
shoe *n.*
shoot *v.*
shop *v.*
shopping *n.*
short *adj.*
shot *n.*
should *modal v.*
shoulder *n.*
shout *v., n.*
show *v., n.*
shower *n.*
shut *v.*
shy *adj.*
sick *adj.*
side *n.*
sight *n.*
sign *n., v.*
signal *n.*
silence *n.*
silly *adj.*
silver *n., adj.*
similar *adj.*
simple *adj.*
since *prep., conj., adv.*
sing *v.*
singer *n.*
single *adj.*
sink *v.*
sir *n.*
sister *n.*
sit *v.*
situation *n.*
size *n.*
skill *n.*
skin *n.*
skirt *n.*
sky *n.*
sleep *v., n.*
sleeve *n.*
slice *n.*
slide *v.*
slightly *adv.*
slip *v.*
slow *adj.*
slowly *adv.*
small *adj.*
smell *v., n.*
smile *v., n.*

smoke *n., v.*
smooth *adj.*
   smoothly *adv.*
snake *n.*
snow *n., v.*
so *adv., conj.*
soap *n.*
social *adj.*
society *n.*
sock *n.*
soft *adj.*
soil *n.*
soldier *n.*
solid *adj., n.*
solution *n.*
solve *v.*
some *adj., pron.*
somebody *pron.*
somehow *adv.*
someone *pron.*
something *pron.*
sometimes *adv.*
somewhere *adv.*
son *n.*
song *n.*
soon *adv.*
   as soon as
sore *adj.*
sorry *adj.*
sort *n., v.*
sound *n., v.*
soup *n.*
south *n., adj., adv.*
southern *adj.*
space *n.*
speak *v.*
speaker *n.*
special *adj.*
speech *n.*
speed *n.*
spell *v.*
spend *v.*
spice *n.*
spider *n.*
spirit *n.*
spoil *v.*
spoon *n.*
sport *n.*
spot *n.*
spread *v.*
spring *n.*
square *adj., n.*
stage *n.*
stair *n.*
stamp *n.*
stand *v., n.*
standard *n., adj.*
star *n.*
stare *v.*

start *v., n.*
state *n., v.*
statement *n.*
station *n.*
stay *v.*
steady *adj.*
steal *v.*
steam *n.*
step *n., v.*
stick *v., n.*
sticky *adj.*
still *adv., adj.*
stomach *n.*
stone *n.*
stop *v., n.*
store *n., v.*
storm *n.*
story *n.*
stove *n.*
straight *adv., adj.*
strange *adj.*
street *n.*
strength *n.*
stress *n.*
stretch *v.*
strict *adj.*
string *n.*
strong *adj.*
strongly *adv.*
structure *n.*
struggle *v., n.*
student *n.*
study *n., v.*
stuff *n.*
stupid *adj.*
style *n.*
subject *n.*
substance *n.*
succeed *v.*
success *n.*
successful *adj.*
successfully *adv.*
such *adj.*
 such as
suck *v.*
sudden *adj.*
suddenly *adv.*
suffer *v.*
sugar *n.*
suggest *v.*
suggestion *n.*
suit *n.*
suitable *adj.*
sum *n.*
summer *n.*
sun *n.*
supply *n.*
support *n., v.*
suppose *v.*

sure *adj., adv.*
surface *n.*
surprise *n., v.*
surprised *adj.*
surround *v.*
survive *v.*
swallow *v.*
swear *v.*
sweat *n., v.*
sweet *adj.*
swim *v.*
switch *n., v.*
symbol *n.*
system *n.*

T

table *n.*
tail *n.*
take *v.*
talk *v., n.*
tall *adj.*
tape *n.*
task *n.*
taste *n., v.*
tax *n.*
tea *n.*
teach *v.*
teacher *n.*
team *n.*
tear /tɛr/ *v.*
tear /tɪr/ *n.*
technical *adj.*
technology *n.*
telephone *n.*
television *n.*
tell *v.*
temperature *n.*
temporary *adj.*
tend *v.*
terrible *adj.*
test *n., v.*
text *n.*
than *prep., conj.*
thank *v.*
thanks *n.*
thank you *n.*
that *adj., pron., conj.*
the *definite article*
theater *n.*
their *adj.*
theirs *pron.*
them *pron.*
themselves *pron.*
then *adv.*
there *adv.*
therefore *adv.*
they *pron.*
thick *adj.*
thin *adj.*

thing *n.*
think *v.*
thirsty *adj.*
this *adj., pron.*
though *conj., adv.*
thought *n.*
thread *n.*
threat *n.*
threaten *v.*
throat *n.*
through *prep., adv.*
throw *v.*
thumb *n.*
ticket *n.*
tie *v., n.*
tight *adj., adv.*
time *n.*
tire *n.*
tired *adj.*
title *n.*
to *prep., infinitive marker*
today *adv., n.*
toe *n.*
together *adv.*
toilet *n.*
tomato *n.*
tomorrow *adv., n.*
tongue *n.*
tonight *adv., n.*
too *adv.*
tool *n.*
tooth *n.*
top *n., adj.*
topic *n.*
total *adj., n.*
totally *adv.*
touch *v., n.*
tour *n.*
tourist *n.*
toward *prep.*
towel *n.*
town *n*
toy *n.*
track *n.*
tradition *n.*
traffic *n.*
train *n., v.*
training *n.*
translate *v.*
transparent *adj.*
transportation *n.*
trash *n.*
travel *v., n.*
treat *v.*
treatment *n.*
tree *n.*
trial *n.*
trick *n.*
trip *n., v.*

trouble *n.*
truck *n.*
true *adj.*
trust *n., v.*
truth *n.*
try *v.*
tube *n.*
tune *n.*
tunnel *n.*
turn *v., n.*
TV *n.*
twice *adv.*
twist *v.*
type *n., v.*
typical *adj.*

U

ugly *adj.*
unable *adj.*
uncle *n.*
uncomfortable *adj.*
unconscious *adj.*
under *prep., adv.*
underground *adj., adv.*
understand *v.*
underwater *adj., adv.*
underwear *n.*
unemployment *n.*
unexpected *adj.*
unexpectedly *adv.*
unfair *adj.*
unfortunately *adv.*
unfriendly *adj.*
unhappy *adj.*
uniform *n.*
union *n.*
unit *n.*
universe *n.*
university *n.*
unkind *adj.*
unknown *adj.*
unless *conj.*
unlikely *adj.*
unlucky *adj.*
unpleasant *adj.*
until *conj., prep.*
unusual *adj.*
up *adv., prep.*
upper *adj.*
upset *v., adj.*
upstairs *adv., adj.*
upward *adv.*
urgent *adj.*
us *pron.*
use *v., n.*
used *adj.*
used to *modal v.*
useful *adj.*
user *n.*

usual *adj.*
usually *adv.*

V

vacation *n.*
valley *n.*
valuable *adj.*
value *n.*
variety *n.*
various *adj.*
vary *v.*
vegetable *n.*
vehicle *n.*
very *adv.*
video *n.*
view *n.*
violence *n.*
violent *adj.*
virtually *adv.*
visit *v., n.*
visitor *n.*
voice *n.*
volume *n.*
vote *n., v.*

W

wait *v.*
wake (up) *v.*
walk *v., n.*
wall *n.*
want *v.*
war *n.*
warm *adj., v.*
warn *v.*
wash *v.*
waste *v., n., adj.*
watch *v., n.*
water *n.*
wave *n., v.*
way *n.*
we *pron.*
weak *adj.*
weakness *n.*
weapon *n.*
wear *v.*
weather *n.*
website *n.*
wedding *n.*
week *n.*
weekend *n.*
weigh *v.*
weight *n.*
welcome *v.*
well *adv., adj., exclamation*
   as well (as)
west *n., adj., adv.*
western *adj.*
wet *adj.*
what *pron., adj.*

whatever *adj., pron., adv.*
wheel *n.*
when *adv., conj.*
whenever *conj.*
where *adv., conj.*
wherever *conj.*
whether *conj.*
which *pron., adj.*
while *conj., n.*
white *adj., n.*
who *pron.*
whoever *pron.*
whole *adj., n.*
whose *adj., pron.*
why *adv.*
wide *adj.*
wife *n.*
wild *adj.*
will *modal v., n.*
win *v.*
wind /wɪnd/ *n.*
window *n.*
wine *n.*
wing *n.*
winner *n.*
winter *n.*
wire *n.*
wish *v., n.*
with *prep.*
within *prep.*
without *prep.*
woman *n.*
wonder *v.*
wonderful *adj.*
wood *n.*
wooden *adj.*
wool *n.*
word *n.*
work *v., n.*
worker *n.*
world *n.*
worried *adj.*
worry *v.*
worse *adj., adv.*
worst *adj., adv., n.*
worth *adj.*
would *modal v.*
wrap *v.*
wrist *n.*
write *v.*
writer *n.*
writing *n.*
wrong *adj., adv.*

Y

yard *n.*
year *n.*
yellow *adj., n.*
yes *exclamation*

yesterday *adv., n.*
yet *adv.*
you *pron.*
young *adj.*
your *adj.*
yours *pron.*
yourself *pron.*
youth *n.*